The Ultimate
Customer Experience!

The Ultimate Customer Experience!

The Path to Victory for Any Business…Any Size…Any Time

ART SURIANO

authorHOUSE®

AuthorHouse™ LLC
1663 Liberty Drive
Bloomington, IN 47403
www.authorhouse.com
Phone: 1-800-839-8640

Published by AuthorHouse   04/30/2014

ISBN: 978-1-4969-0929-9 (sc)
ISBN: 978-1-4969-0928-2 (e)

Any people depicted in stock imagery provided by Thinkstock are
models, and such images are being used for illustrative purposes only.
Certain stock imagery © Thinkstock.

This book is printed on acid-free paper.

Because of the dynamic nature of the Internet, any web
addresses or links contained in this book may have changed
since publication and may no longer be valid. The views
expressed in this work are solely those of the author and do
not necessarily reflect the views of the publisher, and the
publisher hereby disclaims any responsibility for them.

I've had the profound pleasure of working with Art and his team at TSi since 2007, when our business at DXLG was about to undertake updating the company's field sales culture. The goal was to focus more on customer service and less on task-driven functions, which dominated a large portion of the sales staff's time. At the time, DXLG did not have a dedicated training department; therefore TSi was hired to create and execute training programs.

Essentially, DXLG followed the principles outlined in The *Ultimate* Customer Experience, which is full of pragmatic practices to improve any retailer's customer service. As all businesses are aware, providing excellent customer service is critical in gaining a competitive edge. As you follow Art's step-by-step approach, you may find yourself referring back to specific chapters along the way. Utilizing these "recipes" for success will improve upon your organization's concept of The *Ultimate* Customer Experience.

—Dennis Hernreich
Former Executive Vice President, Chief Financial Officer and Chief Operating Officer Destination XL Group, Inc.

Art Suriano is the author of a new book, The *Ultimate* Customer Experience. This book belongs on the desk, iPad, or on the Kindle of every CEO and business manager who is in retail, or any other industry that relies heavily on a positive customer experience to promote the growth of their enterprise.

Art outlines a series of "mini-lessons" that can easily be incorporated into the development of a company's staff and personnel. What makes this book valuable and full of insight is the genuine approach that Art takes concerning a subject that is often reduced down to metrics and statistics. Art's genuine approach to effectively running a business and teaching his clients is demonstrated throughout each chapter.

—J.P. Sakey
President & CEO
Headway Workforce Solutions, Inc.

The *ULTIMATE* Customer Experience!

The Path to Victory for Any Business . . . Any Size . . . Any Time

Contributing Editors: Tricia Rubino and Joanne Del Greco

Cover Concept and Subtitle: Tricia Rubino and Joanne DelGreco

Cover Design by Tiffany Jachera

To my wife Janet,

whose patience and belief in me has made all things possible on our journey together.

Acknowledgments

There are many people who deserve my thanks, not only for their contributions to the experiences that led to this book, but for setting the compass in my life and puffing wind into my sail. Without these special people, I could never have shared what I've learned.

First and foremost, I thank God, my Heavenly Father, who blesses me every day and makes "all" things possible. Thanks to my parents Eleanor and Arthur for their guidance and wisdom; my sister, Joanne, for always being there for me; and my children, David and Stephanie, who motivate me to keep on moving forward.

Thank you to those who inspired me to write this book, Ray Radleigh and Matt Moran; and special thanks to Tricia Rubino for her contributions to this project. Also, Tiffany Jachera for her fine cover designs, and all those at The TSi Company who make our business fun and exciting. Lastly, thanks to all the people through the years who I have been able to call my "friends."

Contents

Foreword

I have spent a career stabilizing, turning around and growing businesses. Currently I am CEO of Orchard Brands Corp., where we serve boomer and senior customers through our catalogs, websites and retail stores; brands include: Blair.com, Haband.com, Drapers.com, NormThompson.com, Solutions.com, Appleseeds.com, Sahalie.com, TogShop.com and GoldViolin.com. Throughout my career, I have had the pleasure of managing several great consumer brands including Lane Bryant and Catherine's (CEO, Charming Shoppes/ now part of Ascena Retail Group); Mueller's, Golden Grain, Pennsylvania Dutch (CEO, American Italian Pasta Company/ now part of the Conagra Group); Levi's and Dockers (CFO, Levi Strauss & Co); Calvin Klein Jeans, Calvin Klein Underwear, Speedo and Chaps (CFO, The Warnaco Group/ now part of Phillips Van Heusen).

I have known Art Suriano for several years and have been a client twice. Art and I met as an outgrowth of my own business evaluation, as I was seeking to better connect with my consumer. I had read of Art's success with another retailer, improving store conversion through his patented methodology. In addition to his passion for the customer, Art understands the importance of front-line employees in any organization. By introducing a "customer first" mentality, Art has successfully repositioned employee performance.

If you have picked up this book, then like me, you recognize the quest for The *Ultimate* Customer Experience as the door to a more profitable business. Like many of you, I have read my share of business books, including several pertaining to the customer. I have also worked with many consulting firms. However, in this book, you will see a focus on one thing only—the customer experience. What you won't get is a lot of consulting-type jargon. You will receive applicable, feasible solutions to the ever-growing customer service problem.

So do you want to deliver a phenomenal customer experience? Are you asking, how will this book do that? Like most things in life, your success will still begin with your execution, but Art's book delivers a roadmap to help get you there. However, if you are the type of person who tends to bottle up problems and pretend that your organization is "ace" at all times, in all areas, then don't waste your time on this book. On the other hand, if you're like me, and you love to question why something is a certain way and desire to see change, then this is the book for you.

The *Ultimate* Customer Experience journey begins early on, as Art throws a "wet blanket" over everyday customer experiences. The customer is literally imploring, "Can you please help me?" and the employee responds, "Well if it's not there, that must mean we are out of it." Art points out the sad truth that while top executives may preach "Customer First," the reality is that the front-line often displays a significant disconnect. Chapter Two delves deeper into organizational disconnect, exemplifying poor customer service. But it also reveals the beginning of a solution: an assessment tool to determine disconnect within any organization. And best of all, the assessment form is laid out for you from A-Z. With disconnect understood and solutions underway, Art moves on to the next building block in Chapters Three through Chapter Five, creating a customer culture that begins with leadership and funnels down to the front-line. And yes, once again Art gives you the assessment form, which can be applied to any business, regardless of size or industry.

Wisely, additional chapters include the employee experience as well. A fully-engaged employee is far better situated to deliver The *Ultimate* Customer Experience, rather than one who is disillusioned. I love Chapter Six—here Art describes the "half baked" customer fixes many companies deploy when hiding behind a "name du jour" such as, "Customer First," "Customer Success," "The Customer Is Our Guest," or "Be Our Guest." These programs are often rolled out through Human Resources or an in-house training staff, and can be poorly communicated to front-line employees.

The book also covers the proper way to conduct "training." Many customer-based business books do not spend time on training. Art displays how effective training is the vehicle that will consistently propel positive customer experiences. Maintaining consistency is key in running a successful company.

The *Ultimate* Customer Experience "journey" never really ends because as business owners or managers, we continue to strive for excellence. Nonetheless, this book winds down with the significance of having passion for your business, as well as the importance of hiring employees that will not only represent your brand, but will build customer loyalty.

If all businesses operate in this manner, success in the form of loyal customers and profit increase are on the way!

Jim Fogarty
Chief Executive Officer, Orchard Brands
Mount Kisco, New York, 2014

Introduction

The Customer Experience

81% of companies with strong capabilities and competencies for delivering customer experience excellence are outperforming their competition.
Source: 2013 Buffer

It is Saturday morning. John has been thinking about a particular item all week and is looking forward to finally purchasing it. He gets up, showers, gets dressed, has a light breakfast, and heads to the mall. It must be *his* day, thinking to himself as he quickly finds a place to park. John walks into the store and heads over to where the item should be. Unfortunately, he cannot find it.

Hmm . . . looking around for help, he thinks to himself,

"Surely there must be someone working here who can help me."

But as John continues to look around, searching for any associate . . . he doesn't see a soul. His first impulse is to shout out . . .

"Is anybody here?"

He wonders to himself . . . how can a store that is open for business, not have any associates available to help customers? Then at last . . . John sees an associate at the register, but his frustration quickly grows, because the cashier has 5 people in line, and John is not about to wait that long to ask a question.

John is not quite ready to give up, so he proceeds to walk around the store looking for someone . . . _ANYONE_ that could help him. Finally . . . John spots a store associate who sees him as well. John is thrilled . . . help at last!

But just as John starts to walk over to him, the associate practically runs the other way and dashes through a door that reads, "Employees Only."

At this point John is extremely upset, wondering why a store associate would run away from a customer. After all, John is convinced the store associate saw him. Once again, John is seriously thinking about shouting as loud as he could . . . "Is anybody here?"

Instead, John decides to give it one last try. He continues to walk around the store, searching for help. He sees another store associate stocking shelves. This time John uses a clever move and quietly sneaks up on the associate, making sure she doesn't see him. "There's no way this person is getting away from me," he says to himself. Then, John makes his move and approaches the store associate.

"Excuse me," John says politely,

"Can you please help me? I am trying to find an item. I went to the correct department, and found several brands and models, but not the one I am looking for. According to the store's ad, you carry the item and it's on sale."

John can't wait for this store associate's answer and assistance! But much to John's surprise, the store associate looks up at John and simply says,

"Well, if it's not there, then the item must be out of stock. Perhaps you can look online."

Then the store associate quickly walks away, dashing into the secret room marked: "Employees Only." John is beside himself and leaves the store. He eventually buys the item from a competitor, vowing never to go back to that store again.

If this situation sounds a little too close to home, then read on as we uncover why this problem occurs, why it's often overlooked and how to solve it. This book provides a detailed outline, which demonstrates how to achieve The *Ultimate* Customer Experience, by building the proper business culture, motivating your employees, and teaching them that no one, or nothing, is more important than the customer.

Businesses today have become whizzes in quickly opening new retail stores, bank branches, auto dealerships, insurance offices, health facilities and restaurants. They have become experts at presenting the biggest and best selection of merchandise, new technology and automated services or food. They have become geniuses in keeping prices competitive, but they have forgotten the most important person who is responsible for making their businesses successful: "The Customer."

In my thirty-plus years of experience, I have been privileged to provide business solutions for some of the best retailers, grocers, restaurants, convenience stores, service companies, manufacturers and distributors in the industry. Many of my clients have been featured in various TOP 100 Lists in their categories. In addition, the services I have provided have ranged from advertising and marketing to training and consulting. However, the main reason I am qualified to write this book is simply this: "I AM A CONSUMER!"

I have been that consumer described above. I have also been the loyal customer who has refused to shop anywhere else when treated appropriately. Furthermore, I have been the customer who has gone out of his way to let others know when NOT to shop at a store because of a terrible experience. I am the person who tells family and friends not to patronize a restaurant, or not to buy from a particular manufacturer due to poor service. The majority of customers, both male and female, only want one simple thing, something I call, "The *Ultimate* Customer Experience."

This book is suited for any company that sells to a customer. No matter what type of business you have, this book is designed to help you satisfy customers, not drive them away. More importantly, you will build brand loyalty by turning satisfied customers into loyal customers who will continue to do business with your company. No matter the size of your company, you can achieve true customer satisfaction.

And most of all, you will learn how your customers can become your best salespeople. Loyal customers help bring in additional business, simply because they offer the best type of advertising that money could never buy . . . *word of mouth*. People listen to their families and friends. So make certain your customers can brag about their great purchase(s) and proudly talk about the outstanding service they received; remember this point, and customers will be doing business with you by the droves. By and large, this type of advertising does not cost you a cent.

Before we begin, let me share a little information about my background. I began my career right out of college, working in advertising, writing jingles, buying media and creating fresh new ad campaigns. Soon I had my own ad agency, developing full campaigns designed for print, radio and television, which gave me the fundamentals to build strong, long-term business relationships. Through the years, I expanded into radio media consulting for some of the largest broadcast companies in the nation.

My role soon became "Mr. Fix It," as I successfully prevented radio stations from losing clients due to poor advertising content. The mission was simply to recreate a new campaign, write and produce new commercials and make sure the campaign was effective. Fortunately, it worked every time.

By the mid 1990's, I founded The TSi Company, now in its twenty-first year. The business began as an in-store music and messaging company, but after discovering the need for store level training, TSi soon expanded.

Today, a very successful TSi offers customized solution services and utilizes a patented methodology known as LTraining®. TSi clients have achieved double-digit comparable store sale increases, as well as high increases in conversion. Working for all types of businesses, TSi implements solutions ranging from marketing and technology to communication and training. TSi's success comes from one principal activity: LISTENING to clients. TSi exercises the ability to recognize customer problems and quickly solve them by building The *Ultimate* Customer Experience.

In this book, we first address the root of all issues: disconnect. This problem often exists between high-level executives and front-line employees. An executive's vision or company mission statement can become diluted as it moves through the ranks. By the time the vision reaches front-line employees, who interact daily with customers, the result is disconnect. Therefore what is actually taking place between employees and customers is something completely different than the original company vision.

Another topic covered is employee empowerment. By giving employees the necessary skills to do their jobs more effectively, performance and productivity are improved, which ultimately increases revenue. In addition, we will discuss communication and training; it is crucial that synergy exists between your external message and your internal message. Your external message is communicated through advertising and marketing, while your internal message is communicated to your employees; in turn, your employees deliver this message to your customers through daily interaction.

This synergy is vital for your company, and it begins with proper training that creatively reinforces the culture of your business. Other areas of discussion include: employee accountability, and the importance of aligning your company's culture with your goals and visions. Another important element is passion; the passion you have for your business should be the driving force of your success.

If you are ready to take your business to the next level, regardless of the success you've already achieved, it begins with a clear understanding of how important the customer is, and placing that customer first. If you truly believe this, you are on your way to increasing sales and profits.

So let's take a look at the first step of how to achieve The *Ultimate* Customer Experience.

Chapter One

The Disconnect

89% of consumers have stopped doing business with a company after experiencing poor customer service. Source: RightNow Customer Experience Impact Report

In my thirty-five years of working for all types of business leaders, I have never met anyone who felt that customer service is unimportant. In fact, CEOs and high-level executives have wholeheartedly told me how passionate they are about the customer, and how vital outstanding service is for the success of their business. These executives create all kinds of programs like "Customer First" and "The Customer Matters Most." However, these programs often fail because the problem is usually not found at the top. Rather, disconnect exists between the vision and objectives of the CEO and the front-line employees, who interact with the customers.

Every type of business deals with customers. How those customers are treated is what makes one business more successful than another. Even if your company is business-to-business and does not serve the general public, you still have customers to serve and they expect a quality experience when they interact with your company.

I'd like to share with you a letter that I sent to a local restaurant a few years ago when a server accidentally spilled sauce on my trousers. Before I explain what took place after I sent the letter, decide as a business owner or manager what you would have done in this situation.

May 18, 2009

Mr. Frank Smith
Manager
Main Street Eatery
123 Main Street
Somewhere, USA

Dear Frank,

I'm contacting you to share an experience that my family and I had at your restaurant last night. Attached, please find a copy of my receipt.

My family and I dine often at your restaurant. As usual, the food was great, the atmosphere pleasant, and the wait minimal. All of these benefits are a credit to your fine establishment, especially since this time we had a party of nine with us. However, because of the quality you offer and knowing how important it is to establish a good "Customer Experience," I felt compelled to write this letter.

My wife and I both ordered the Grilled Lemon Pepper Chicken. It was quite good. However, upon receiving my plate, the server spilled some of the sauce from the plate on to my trousers. I completely understand that things happen. Politely, I immediately called her attention to it. However, her reaction surprised me when she did nothing, so I asked her for a wet cloth. She just looked at me and walked away, focusing on other tables. Finally, I got her attention again and asked for some seltzer. Eventually she brought me the seltzer and I was able to get a cloth from her as well. Yet, she never once acknowledged that she spilled sauce on my trousers.

We continued eating the meal even though my pants were now stained; since we were celebrating a birthday with a large group of people, we ordered dessert as well. I was most disappointed that during the remainder of the meal, there was no apology or offer to pay for dry cleaning. Worst of all, on the bill was a charge for the seltzer.

As I mentioned earlier, you have a fine restaurant, but this type of service will not help you grow your business. Now as a customer, I am not sure I will return, fearing I might once again receive the same type of careless service. Had the server offered to pay for the dry cleaning, I would have not accepted because I understand that accidents can happen. However, her attitude and lack of concern did not give us a good "Customer Experience."

Frank, I have sent you this letter so that you are aware of the situation. As a business owner myself, I would always want to know if any of my employees did something that negatively affected any of our clients.

Very truly yours,
Art Suriano

So if you were the manager of this restaurant and received my letter, what would you have done? Would you have attempted to reach the customer? Would you have written a reply? Would you have extended an offer to invite the customer to come back? The choices may seem obvious; however, this is what happened . . .

I sent the letter certified mail to make sure the restaurant received it. When I received the green card from the post office, I saw that Frank himself had signed for the letter. Well, it has been almost five years and I never received a response.

Up until this experience, we would frequent that restaurant at least three or four times a year with groups of eight to fifteen people, but instead, none of us returned. Think of the lost business; for almost five years now, we have enjoyed our family dinners out at another restaurant and have made it the new special gathering place.

Do you think the owner of the restaurant ever learned about my letter? My intuition tells me no.

To me, the issue was disconnect, which existed between the owner's vision about service and what was happening at Frank's location. Frank probably received the letter, may or may not have even read it, placed it somewhere and forgot all about it. Maybe that day, Frank had other responsibilities to deal with, which he felt were more important than the customer—that was a big mistake. The final point I want to make is this: By ignoring the opportunity to change a negative experience into a positive one, Frank not only made the situation worse, he also lost customers. Again, I ask, who is more important than the customer?

By now you should be asking yourself this question: "How do I find disconnect between my expectations about service, and the type of service that my employees are providing to my customers?" This is the first step that needs to be identified clearly, so that we can implement the strategy to correct it.

We will begin with a comprehensive assessment that can be customized for any business. The assessment provides valuable information, which can be used to fix any disconnect you may uncover.

The *Ultimate* Customer Experience:

Step One—The Assessment

Every CEO needs to know the vision of his or her business, including long and short-term goals. Begin by making sure that you have a clear understanding of where your business currently is and where you want it to go. Start with at least three objectives that you wish to accomplish over the next year, and then continue with future objectives over the next three to five years. Simply saying, "I want more sales," is not enough. For example, if you are a business with 50 locations, do you dream of expanding into 200 locations? Make sure not to overstate your expectations with something that is impractical. For example, your company is currently generating 5 million a year in sales, but your aspiration is to be a 200 billion dollar business in five years. A goal such as this may be quite unrealistic.

Below are examples of two different companies that established a vision and outlined their goals:

Charlie's Floral Shop: A chain of 100 floral retailers

Vision: Become the leading, Midwestern floral chain, known for outstanding customer service and satisfaction

Short-Term Goals (This Year): Hire two new district managers; open two new stores; re-vamp custom floral arrangements department

Long-Term Goals (Five Years): Open 3-5 new stores a year for the next five years; expand mobile marketing, allowing custom arrangements to be created online and picked up at the store; expand same day free delivery throughout the chain

The owner of Charlie's Floral Shop has an easy-to-understand vision of becoming the leading floral chain in the Midwest. Additionally, the owner addresses how he will achieve his vision—it will come from how his employees treat and satisfy his customers. His short and long-term goals support his vision and contribute to making his dreams become a reality.

Let's take a look at another company's vision and goals outline:

Mail Or Market Direct-MMD: A direct marketing firm engaged in all types of media for direct response advertising

Vision: Become the leading direct marketing agency, utilizing innovative technology to provide clients with outstanding customer service and unique marketing strategies

Short-Term Goals (This Year): Pilot a new single mailer customization program to at least 500 customers; expand reach into the Hispanic market, and hire two bi-lingual managers; update production studio with new technology

Long-Term Goals (Five Years): Become the leader of a single mailer customization program and the largest direct marketer for both the Hispanic and Asian markets.

Take a moment to complete your vision, as well as your short and long-term goals. Share this information, first with your senior staff, and shortly thereafter with your entire company. If you are in business for yourself, review what you have written down often, in order to keep yourself on course and achieve your goals.

Now that you have identified your vision and your goals, it is time for you to assess your business. Performing an assessment is extremely beneficial. The assessment process begins with a questionnaire that is relevant to your business.

The assessment results will identify the type of interaction that is taking place between your employees and your customers. The questionnaire may also reveal details concerning how customers perceive your business.

As a guideline, this book provides a full assessment questionnaire of thirty important questions. It begins in this chapter and continues through Chapter Four. Remember, you can customize each question according to your type of business.

For the purpose of the assessment, we will continue to use Charlie's Floral Shop. As we go through the questionnaire, think of your company's objectives and how they pertain to these questions. Add or interchange your own questions as you see fit.

Depending on the size of your business, you may or may not be the one conducting the assessment. Only one person should conduct ALL the interviews, and that person should have a clear understanding of your company's goals and vision. Using different interviewers will complicate the process and can have a negative effect on the information you receive. In addition, the same person should organize all the information gathered. This is vital for creating the assessment report, which will contain all the information obtained in an organized manner, after all the interviews are completed.

When presenting the assessment, you should decide whom to interview and create a complete interviewee list. I recommend including your senior staff, as well as the heads of each department. In addition if you operate a retail store, select managers and a few store associates. If you operate a restaurant, include servers, bartenders and hosts. A service business should include supervisory employees who frequently interact with customers, as well as a few front-line employees.

Most importantly, the person conducting the interviews MUST LISTEN closely to the answers. Do not in any way interrupt or attempt to get the interviewee to modify his or her response so that it conforms to your expectations. Keep the assessment interviews and responses anonymous. It is imperative that all interviewees feel comfortable and are honest. Avoid accepting general answers and stay away from asking simple "yes" or "no" questions. Your goal is to encourage interviewees to share information, including their thoughts, opinions, and comments. The more information you obtain, the easier it will be to repair whatever disconnect you may find.

Let's take a look at the first six questions:

ASSESSMENT REVIEW FORM

Name: _____

Title: _____

Length of time and experience with Charlie's Floral Shop: _____

The above information will be kept confidential when reporting survey results.

1. Describe the company vision as delivered by the leaders of the company.

_____
_____
_____

2. What do you feel are the important short-term and long-term goals for Charlie's Floral Shop?

_____
_____
_____

3. When you hear "Charlie's Floral Shop," what image comes to mind?

    _____

    _____

    _____

4. How would your customers describe Charlie's Floral Shop?

    _____

    _____

    _____

5. On a scale of 1-10 (10 being the highest) how would you rate customer service, such as greeting and engaging the customer, and assisting the customer?

    _____

    _____

    _____

6. On a scale of 1-10 (10 being the highest) how would you rate your business regarding inviting the customer back?

    _____

    _____

    _____

Let's review question one and what you should be looking for in your interviewees' responses:

Question One*: Describe the company vision as delivered by the leaders of the company.*

This question is the foundation of your business' growth and ultimate success. It is not essential that those interviewed provide a word-for-word answer, like a quote, although I have experienced that with some businesses. What is important is that the general understanding and principles of the vision be evident in the responses. Every employee from the top to the bottom levels must know and understand what the vision of your company is. If not, this becomes the first problem that you will need to resolve.

Question Two: *What do you feel are the important short-term and long-term goals for Charlie's Floral Shop?*

Although the interviewee may understand the company vision, he or she may not know the short and long-term goals. Conversely, if the interviewee did not understand the company vision, he or she may still know the short and long-term goals. This is because "vision" is a concept, while goals are tangible. Ask questions to see if the interviewee understands the meaning and importance of your goals, instead of just reciting them.

If during the interview process you discover that the interviewee does not agree with your goals, ask for his or her reasons, listen, and allow the individual to feel comfortable sharing them. You would be surprised how many invaluable ideas and suggestions come from the people who work for you and have daily contact with your customers.

You will most likely find that those who work closely under you will know your goals. As you interview those in the lower levels of the chain of command, you will find the responses become very different, and this is where disconnect exists.

Question Three: *When you hear "Charlie's Floral Shop," what image comes to mind?*

This question is often misunderstood. Suppose the front desk associate at a health club is selling memberships and believes that the free day with a trainer is just a way to attract new customers. In reality, the owner provides that service to make sure that patrons use the equipment correctly and do not injure themselves. Those are two completely different messages. The front desk associate is saying to customers interested in signing up, "We give you a personal trainer for one whole day FREE of charge." On the other hand, the owner of the health club cares about providing clients with safe and supervised workouts. Therefore, what should be said is, "We provide a personal trainer your first day at no cost, to make sure you safely get the most out of your workouts." As you can see regarding this question, employees often have mixed messages concerning the company's mission. Employees may be unclear as to the images that come to mind when they hear the company's name. It's imperative that this confusion be cleared up immediately.

Question Four: *How would your customers describe Charlie's Floral Shop?*

This information usually comes from front-line employees who speak directly with customers, however employees may tend to misinterpret what customers are saying, or even what they want.

Remember the example given in the previous question regarding the health spa? It proved employees and management are not always on the same page regarding "why" a promotion or special offer is launched. This also holds true for a customer's perception of a business. I have witnessed situations where customers' views of a business are extremely different than that of the employees.

For example, a customer may only shop a particular store for convenience; perhaps the store is close by, is rarely crowded and has plenty of parking. Nonetheless the customer is not particularly thrilled about the store's merchandise selection. Conversely, if the employee believes the customer shops at the store for quality selection and attractive prices, there is great disconnect concerning company perception.

Question Five: *On a scale of 1-10 (10 being the highest) how would you rate customer service, such as greeting and engaging the customer, and assisting the customer?*

This is the first of many questions we will ask in order to measure how well the customer experience is being provided. Questions like this are an excellent gauge for measuring disconnect, and can often reveal the root of various issues.

Rarely will you find that everyone within the organization is rating the company the same. Typically, company executives tend to give higher scores and the lower scores will come from the front-line employees. However there have been some instances where the scores are reversed, and the front-line rated the company higher than upper management did.

Question Six: *On a scale of 1-10 (10 being the highest) how would you rate your business regarding inviting the customer back?*

This question will help measure how successful you are when inviting customers back to do business with you again. It is critical that all employees who deal directly with customers understand the importance of inviting customers back. Perhaps your company scripted a specific phrase that is mandated for your customer service program. If so, this question will reveal if this phrase is being implemented, and how well it is working. Remember, customer satisfaction must be guaranteed every time and inviting the customer back is an important part of achieving that satisfaction.

A short, but important note about the assessment questions: My firm has been using this process for years, and the common denominator is that no matter how successful companies are, they all seem to suffer from some type of disconnect among different levels of staff.

Recently when performing an assessment for a large company with various locations, we discovered the following: A director, just two levels down from the CEO, who had been with the company for eight years, admitted that he did not know the company's short and long-term goals, and he had absolutely no idea what the CEO's vision was. Now this may seem unusual; however, this type of disconnect has become a major problem in more organizations than you may think.

As the assessment continued and we moved down to the front-line employees, the amount of disconnect discovered was tremendous. Disconnect can occur in any business. Nevertheless, it's evident that the more employees a company has, the greater the opportunity for disconnect to emerge between management and employees. For this reason, it is imperative to catch disconnect issues early on, so they will not spread through the organization like a cancer and ultimately destroy the business.

Chapter Two

The Culture

It takes 12 positive service experiences to make up for one negative experience.
Source: "Understanding Customers" by Ruby Newell-Legner

In addition to repairing company disconnect, another major component for building The *Ultimate* Customer Experience is creating a culture that clearly defines your commitment to the customer. If you truly believe that no one, or nothing, is more important than the customer, everyone in your company must embrace, understand and practice this concept, beginning with you. The culture of your business is what will set you apart from your competitors. Customers flock to businesses that make them feel special. Creating and implementing the right culture for your business will automatically make it much easier to put the customer first, and it's also another building block to great success.

I can usually tell what type of business culture a company has just by sitting in the lobby area, waiting to enter their office for a meeting. How? ... by observing their employees. The first employee I encounter is the receptionist. This person is VERY important; he or she is the first point of contact visitors will have with the company.

The way a receptionist greets guests is vital, and sets the tone for the entire company.

As I sit and wait for my meeting, I watch employees walk by. Just to see their reactions, I deliberately try to make eye contact with a nod and a smile. When they smile or nod back, I know that I'm in a company that has a friendly working environment, but more importantly, a company that has the right business culture. Yet, almost every time an impolite receptionist greets me, I also find employees walking by me in the lobby without any acknowledgement. In fact, those employees tend to walk with their heads down, or they quickly look away and avoid making eye contact.

Conversely, there are businesses that no longer have a receptionist, yet these companies continue to bring customers and vendors into their office.

A word of advice to these businesses: think twice about the money that you believe you are saving. Without a receptionist, the company appears cold and sends a message that it does not care about its customers.

Regardless, if your company primarily interacts with vendors, customer service should be offered throughout all levels of your business. Your vendors may not be your customers in a traditional sense, but they provide you with the commodities needed to sell to your customers. Build strong vendor relationships, which will not only improve company perception, but will also help you negotiate buying options. In summary, if you have a receptionist, make sure he or she is pleasant and represents your company's mission statement. If you no longer have a receptionist, consider reinstating one.

Before we move on, take a moment and be honest with yourself regarding your own interactions with people, not just your employees. When you are out of your office or business location, how do you interact with strangers? This will tell you something about yourself and what type of culture you are creating within your company. For example, perhaps you are at a breakfast or brunch buffet. Are you polite to those around you and to the servers? Do you use words like, "excuse me," "thank you" and, "please?" If not, the culture of your business may not be what you wish it to be. In no way can you have a "do as I say, not as I do" mentality. Remember the old adage, "you can catch more flies with honey than vinegar."

You create the culture, and your entire business is built upon that culture. Begin with yourself and make sure you are treating those around you the way you want to be treated, and most importantly, the way you want your customers to be treated.

I will never forget an experience my wife and I had years ago. While coming home from work one night, she informed me that the washing machine had broken and it was time for a new one. She had already done some research and found the washing machine she wanted, so we went off to a local big box store to make the purchase. It was a Tuesday, which typically is not a busy time for most retailers, and it was raining, so things were even slower. Upon arriving at the store, it was obvious there were hardly any customers inside.

We walked over to the appliance area, and we found the washing machine my wife was interested in purchasing. Almost immediately, we both noted there were two machines that looked exactly alike. Yet, there was a fifty-dollar difference in the price. We looked around for some help and noticed that not too far from us was a person talking on the phone, who appeared to be a store associate. I walked over to him and discovered he was having a personal conversation, so I waited patiently for him to finish. Finally, after getting his attention he came over to the appliance area where my wife had been waiting. He greeted us saying,

"How can I help you?"

I explained to him that we were interested in purchasing the washing machine, but that we were curious what the difference was between the two machines. Unfortunately, we could not ascertain an explanation from the product information tags that might have explained the difference. He looked at us both and said:

"Well I can sell it to you, and I can arrange for delivery, but I don't know anything about washing machines because I usually work in the audio department."

After that statement, he proceeded to leave us standing there and simply walked away. By now my wife and I were a bit angry; it was getting late and our frustration was growing. A few minutes later, we saw another associate walking by, and he clearly stood out. This store's dress code consisted of khaki pants with a blue shirt. However, this associate was also wearing an unbuttoned Hawaiian shirt over his blue shirt. I will never forget his name, Ben, because he was not wearing this store's standard name badge. Instead, he had a piece of masking tape on his shirt with the name "Ben" written on it in black marker. Now how do you forget something like that? I was able to get his attention and he came over to my wife and me and said,

"How can I help you?"

Once again, I explained to him that we were interested in purchasing the washing machine, but we were curious what the difference was between the two machines. We did not read anything on the product information tags that explained the difference between the two machines. He looked at us both and said,

"Well I can sell it you, and I can arrange for delivery, but I don't know anything about washing machines because I usually work in the TV department."

At this point, my wife and I had enough, and we left. The next night I came home early from work and we went to the local appliance store in town. It was a much smaller store and they did not have nearly the same selection as the big box store. Moreover, their prices were a bit higher as well, but they did have the washing machine my wife wanted. Within twenty minutes of speaking with Fred, the nicely dressed, knowledgeable and courteous salesman (wearing a professional name badge) who assisted us, we learned the difference between the two machines. Fred explained that the more expensive model had a heavier belt, and since we had two small children at the time and lots of laundry, Fred recommended we purchase it, and we did.

The new washing machine started out costing $50 more than the big box store, but it turned out that the small appliance store delivered it for free, and the big box store charged $65 for delivery. In addition, the small appliance store offered complimentary removal of the old washing machine, while the other store charged a $25 fee. Through the years we gave that small appliance store all of our business and encouraged our friends and family to shop there, and they did.

After looking at both stores, the big box store did not possess a positive business culture, which exemplified the company's disconnect. Perhaps if only one salesperson brushed us off, it could have been an issue with that particular individual, but when two salespeople virtually say the same exact thing, it reveals something more serious. The culture in that store is distorted, and the mentality is to sell as much as you can to whomever you can, without providing any type of customer assistance. This will *not* produce the *Ultimate* Customer Experience.

There was obviously no product training, no customer service training, and absolutely no evidence of a positive business culture, all necessary components for providing an outstanding customer experience.

Yet, the small appliance store was full of friendly employees. These salespeople took time with my wife and me to make sure we would be pleased with our purchase. There was a positive business culture, which was shared by everyone who worked in the store. They knew how to provide The *Ultimate* Customer Experience.

After reading about these two store experiences, think about the type of culture your business exemplifies. Are you and your employees doing everything possible to make the customer feel welcome? Are you making sure that the customer is happy and satisfied after the purchase? Do you or your associates ever follow up with a customer after a purchase to make sure everything is still satisfactory?

One thing that the small appliance store did still stands out in my mind. The store called me one week after the purchase to make sure the washing machine was working properly and to ask whether I had any other questions. In my case, when they called me, it turned out I also needed a new lawn mower, and I found myself back at that small appliance store buying a lawn mower about an hour after that phone call.

If you are thinking that it is easy for a small appliance store to provide great customer service, but that it is nearly impossible for a chain with hundreds of locations, I suggest you think again. Years ago, I flew into Omaha for a big meeting with a new client. I arrived the night before and the airline destroyed the suit hanger that was in my suitcase. After my meeting, I was flying to another location and wanted to make sure my suit would survive. I was determined to buy a new suit hanger, and I also decided to purchase a new business card case. I had no idea how difficult that would be. That evening I headed over to the mall and decided to tackle the business card case first. Upon arriving, I remembered a store that carried them. While I was very disappointed with the selection, I bought one anyway. Then the search for a wooden suit hanger began. Store after store that sold suits did not sell hangers, and the best I could find were poor quality plastic ones.

Finally, I entered the last department store at the mall, went to the men's suit department, and I asked the saleswoman if they sold wooden suit hangers and explained my situation. The saleswoman in the suit department smiled at me, called over Mike, another store associate, and said,

"Please give this nice customer one of our suit hangers."

I was speechless when she had no intention of charging me for the hanger, especially since I had not purchased anything. While I was waiting for Mike to bring me the hanger, I noticed an expensive leather business card case and purchased it. The two store associates treated me as if I was their only customer, and because of the outstanding service, I made a purchase. It has been four years since I had that experience and every time I use the card case or the hanger, I remember it well.

My point is that this department store chain has several locations and thousands of employees. Yet, even with a business this size, they managed to have a culture that puts the customer first, regardless if a purchase was made.

So think about this carefully . . . how do you assess your current culture? How do you know if you and your employees are on the right track, and aligned with the culture you expect for your business? Let us continue the assessment process that we began in Chapter One by adding additional questions. Take a moment and read through the following questions, which will help you identify the culture of your business:

7. How long have you been working for Charlie's Floral Shop?

    _____

    _____

    _____

8. Do you like your job? If "Yes," please tell us why and if "No," please elaborate on the reasons.

    _____

    _____

    _____

9. Do you feel you are appreciated and recognized for your contribution to the company?

    _____

    _____

    _____

10. Do you like your customers? If so, why and if not, please elaborate.

    _____

    _____

    _____

11. Tell us your best experience in satisfying a customer.

    _____

    _____

    _____

12. Tell us the worst experience you had with a customer.

    _____

    _____

    _____

13. How do you handle getting your tasks done and assisting customers? Explain what you do.

_____

_____

_____

Let's go through the questions and review why we are asking them.

Question Seven: *How long have you been working for Charlie's Floral Shop?*

If the majority of interviewees are stating three years or more, the good news is you are not suffering from high turnover. Long-term employees know more about your business, can provide useful information based on their experience with your company, and are familiar with changes that may have taken place over the years.

Although employees who have only been with the company for a short period of time may not have vast knowledge about your business, they can be more objective. The newer employees can often recognize factors that the long-term employees no longer see, and this is beneficial. So don't be too quick to disregard feedback from new employees.

Question Eight: *Do you like your job? If "Yes," tell us why and if "No," please elaborate on the reasons.*

It is crucial that employees enjoy their jobs. When they do, they automatically show passion for their work, have a desire to do their best, and take pride in what they accomplish. Nonetheless, if employees do not enjoy their job, they may still perform their duties to your satisfaction, but in time, their negative attitude will begin to spread like a malignancy throughout the company, and eventually customers will begin to sense it too.

I will never forget the time when I was doing business with a local auto dealership, and I had gotten to know the owner, Tom, very well. One day Tom was sharing his concerns about his salesperson, Marc, who for some reason could not close a sale. Yet, Tom felt Marc was one of the nicest people one would ever meet.

I asked Tom if he ever inquired as to why Marc became a salesperson. I also said to Tom, "Perhaps Marc isn't right for sales, but maybe there is another position within the dealership that he could excel at." At first, Tom didn't take my advice. However a month later, Tom spent a significant amount of time with Marc, teaching him how to close a sale. Unfortunately, this effort failed and finally Tom asked Marc if he liked his job. Marc thought for a moment, in fear of being fired, and admitted that although he enjoyed working at the dealership, he did not like certain aspects of his job. Tom appreciated Marc's honesty, and proceeded to ask him a few more key questions. Tom soon realized that Marc had a real passion for advertising. The timing of their conversation was perfect; Tom needed to replace his in-house ad person and decided to give Marc a chance. Within 6 months, sales were the strongest they had ever been and it was obvious Marc was the right person for the job. Marc's approach to local auto dealership advertising was the best of any other competitors, and Tom was thrilled by the amount of business the ads were generating.

Question Nine: *Do you feel you are appreciated and recognized for your contribution to the company?*

When using this question as part of the assessment, you would be quite surprised to know how many owners and managers just do not understand it. He or she feels that as long as the employees do their jobs and get a paycheck each week, that is all the appreciation and recognition they need. How wrong is that? Many employees tend to leave their jobs due to a lack of appreciation and recognition, as opposed to leaving over salary issues. Yet, too many employers do not realize it.

However, if employees answer that they do feel appreciated and recognized, it's a reflection of a healthy business culture. Your company may be a business that has recognition programs, which are always a great benefit to provide. I have found that the simplest gesture can go a long way, like printing out a certificate of acknowledgement and presenting it to an employee for exemplary service. Sometimes your managers may come up with their own ideas to provide ways of thanking their employees for great service, such as complimentary meals, attending a sporting event or another type of group activity.

If the interviewee does not feel appreciated or recognized, again, listen and find out why. Often good service goes unrecognized and a great employee may find work elsewhere. Remember, it takes more time and money to hire and to train new employees than it does to recognize the good ones you already have.

Question Ten: *Do you like your customers? If so, why and if not, please elaborate.*

If your employees' answer to this question is "yes," take it a step further and ask them to elaborate as to why they like your customers. You should hear comments like, "they are very friendly," "they really appreciate my help," and "they listen to my recommendations." Those types of responses let you know that your employee is doing a good job satisfying your customers. If the employee says, "yes" and gives answers like, "because they don't hassle me," or "they don't take too much of my time," this employee clearly does not understand the meaning of customer service, and is not part of the culture you would like them to emulate.

Worse yet, if the interviewee gives any indication that he or she does not like your customers, it can be for a variety of reasons, but most often it will be that the employee is wrong for the job. However, there could be some issues that you need to address, such as the employee feeling overworked from having too many tasks, and so he or she believes that customers are taking up too much time. As a result, the manager holds the employee responsible for not completing those tasks on time. If that is the case, and it happens quite often in businesses with disconnect between corporate and lower management, then it should be addressed and repaired quickly.

Question Eleven: *Tell us your best experience in satisfying a customer.*

Every employee who interacts with customers should be able to cite several positive experiences. Employees should easily have their favorite, if not multiple favorite stories to share. These stories can also be used to encourage other employees. However, if the interviewee has no positive experiences to share, continue to encourage him or her to elaborate; based on the reasons given, you will have to decide if this person is right for the position.

Question Twelve*: Tell us the worst experience you had with a customer.*

Caring employees become troubled when they have an unpleasant customer experience. Often it is not their fault, but they are upset when it happens and they always remember the experience.

You may learn from an employee's answer that the experience went sour because the situation was beyond the employee's control. For example, a customer purchased something that was damaged during delivery. The store wants to repair it rather than replace it, and the customer is unhappy. The disgruntled customer comes back into the store and lets the salesperson know how unhappy he or she is, and tells the salesperson, "I will NEVER do business with this store again."

In this case it was not the employee's fault, but instead, it was simply the store policy.

Another negative experience occurs when the employee gives the customer a price quoted by the store manager for either merchandise or product insurance, but when the order is entered into the system, the employee learns that the price he or she quoted was incorrect because of an internal miscommunication. Now the employee has to tell the customer that the original price quoted was incorrect, and the customer is undoubtedly upset with the employee. When these experiences occur, your employees take the brunt of the responsibility because they deal directly with the customer. When management does not pay attention to these incidents, or attempt to resolve them, not only are customers lost, but valuable employees are lost as well.

Question Thirteen: *How do you handle getting your tasks done and assisting customers? Explain what you do.*

Employees who interact with customers are also responsible for performing other tasks. We are all familiar with the store associate who is accomplishing his or her task while the customer is waiting to be serviced. Successful businesses have taught their employees that the customer always comes first, and the other tasks should be completed after the customer is satisfied. However, that often sounds too good to be true. In many businesses, the pressure of completing tasks gets in the way of providing outstanding customer service.

When asking this question, find out if the interviewee is successfully managing his or her time, and understands that the customer comes before anything else. If the answer is no, find out what is hindering his or her ability to multi-task.

Consequently as in question twelve, there may be circumstances taking place that are completely beyond the control of the employee.

Chapter Three

Balancing The Internal and External Message

Attracting a new customer costs 5 times as much as keeping an existing one.
Source: Lee Resource Inc.

Your company's internal and external message must be one and the same.

Misaligned internal and external communication sends confusing messages to customers and wastes advertising dollars.

To attract customers, businesses use external advertising such as radio, television, newspaper, direct mail, and the Internet. Subsequently, internal marketing's main role is to support what the business promotes through its advertising, so when customers respond, front-line employees are ready to take action.

Advertising is expensive, therefore internal and external marketing must work in unison to ensure that a clear and consistent message is delivered to the customer. Effective marketing drives traffic to the business and brings in repeat customers, ultimately increasing sales.

Most retailers, restaurants and service businesses use coupons, sales, discounts, special events, and other promotions to generate sales. Retailers have also expanded promotions to include events such as a "One Day Sale," "Buy One Get One," also known as BOGO, "Christmas In July" and "Beach Party" in January.

Some retailers have even created their own programs, whereby customers can receive either money back or points, which can be used towards future purchases.

But what happens when a customer is not able to benefit from the promotion that a company advertised? When this occurs the customer is confused, frustrated, and often leaves. This not only costs the company sales, it also does not provide a positive customer experience. What causes this to happen? Once again, it is disconnect; this time it is between the marketing and operations departments.

I remember receiving a direct mail piece from a popular restaurant chain promoting a "Buy One Entrée, Get A Second Entrée Half Off." I took my family to the restaurant and we had a pleasant meal; however when the check came, I gave the server the direct mail piece and he knew nothing about the promotion. The server brought the manager over to our table to resolve the issue. The manager apologized and explained that this location was not involved in the promotion, so there was nothing that he could do to honor the discount. We paid full price for the meal, and never went back to that restaurant. Nowhere on the direct mail piece did it say, "at participating locations only," nor did it provide any disclaimer. Why would a restaurant chain spend all that money advertising, and not provide a disclaimer for the customer, as well as notification to the restaurant's other franchises?

Now let's look at a common issue among service businesses. There are some service businesses that constantly hound consumers with direct mail pieces, phone calls and emails, asking them for their business, which they already have.

For example, a satellite radio company that I have been subscribing to for ten years continues to send me volumes of direct mail, asking me to open an account for a vehicle I no longer drive. This demonstrates that the company is not familiar with their current customer base. Furthermore, I realized that since I'm paying monthly service fees, I am also supporting this pointless advertising.

Again, it is critical that the internal and external message is clear, and addresses only those customers who can gain value from the offer. Most importantly, the external message must be aligned with the internal operations of that business. Let's take a look at what happens when this is not the case, and the problems that can result from disconnect.

As businesses grow, each department becomes fixated on task completion, and easily loses sight of the bigger picture: the company vision.

For example, often the marketing and advertising departments are primarily focused on their media deadlines and what promotional offer they can create. These departments primarily work alongside other internal departments, ensuring every detail of the promotion will be executed, especially the kick-off date. While this initiative is important, it is equally important to ensure front-line employees are completely familiar with the offer and its purpose.

Suppose a car rental facility produced a special weekend promotion offering its club members half off on all prestige rentals. The marketing department developed the promotional collateral and met all deadlines for a direct mail and newspaper campaign; the operations department assured available inventory. However, communication to the sales reps at the rental facilities was lacking, and as a result, the representatives had no knowledge of how to handle the promotion. The outcome: dissatisfied customers and less than favorable sales figures.

The company could have easily improved the promotion's success if they had fully communicated the details to their sales reps, as well as the reason *why* they were offering club members half price rentals for the weekend. By offering customers an opportunity to drive these cars and enjoy them on a trial basis, some customers would no doubt rethink which vehicle they choose to rent in the future. However, because of disconnect, the promotion did not reach its full potential.

When implementing a promotional offer, most businesses will attempt to create some type of internal communication. Perhaps corporate will send an email to a manager or regional director, and that person will be responsible for informing employees. Companies who consistently offer promotions will most likely post a copy of the offer in the employee breakroom. Promotional details will be discussed, possibly during the morning staff meeting. Often what is typically covered in the meeting is the promotional offer itself, but direction may not be given on how to turn the offer into an amazing customer experience.

For example, have you ever walked into a restaurant, only to be greeted with a canned line like,

"Hello. Thank you for dining at Joe's Restaurant. Today we're offering seven different appetizers for only $4.95 each!"

After being seated, the server walks over and repeats the same line,

"Hello, my name is Josh. Thank you for dining today at Joe's Restaurant . . . today we're offering seven different appetizers for only $4.95 each!"

Wow, overwhelming! What ever happened to giving patrons a minute to settle in at the table and order drinks before reciting specials?

Do you think a customer who is greeted in that manner is having a favorable customer experience? If you think not, please read on.

If you attended a dinner party, wouldn't you expect to receive a friendly greeting, along with an invitation to come inside and sit down? Then perhaps the host might offer you a beverage before dining. Conversely, would the host immediately jump in front of you the minute you walked through the door, with some rehearsed line, rattling off what beverages you could have with dinner? If that were the case, how would you feel? Pressured? Uncomfortable? A little confused? Of course you would. Remember . . . customers are people just like you, and if treated right, they will look forward to returning. This means repeat business. Remember, satisfied customers will spread the news of their great experiences to friends and family.

In the case of the restaurant that offered the appetizer promotion, here is a better approach that will generate successful results. The customer walks in and is greeted by the host who says,

"Hello and welcome to Joe's Restaurant . . . we're pleased to see you. Your server is looking forward to sharing some great appetizer offers. Let me seat you and make you comfortable."

A few minutes after the host seats the customers, the server greets them and says,

"Hello, my name is Josh and I'll be your server today. May I take your drink order and tell you about today's great offer on appetizers?"

The customer is almost never going to say no. This approach makes the customer more relaxed and better able to pay further attention to the offers. The customer will be provided with an enjoyable experience, and most likely the restaurant will sell more appetizers.

Using once again Joe's Restaurant and the appetizer promotion, the managers should also explain the offer to their staff, including what appetizers are being offered for only $4.95, as well as *why* they are offering the appetizer specials.

Yes, Joe's Restaurant wants to increase sales, but the customer is not going to care about that. There can be any number of reasons why this promotion might be offered, but it's important to point out to the staff the *why* factor. Here is an example that management could use when explaining the importance of *why* a customer would find a promotion attractive.

"Our research shows that our customers like the appetizers we offer, but don't like spending the extra money. Today's offer is giving them an opportunity to try an appetizer at a discounted price. We would like them to enjoy it so much that they will order it again on their next visit. In addition, some of our appetizers are offered as full entrées, so if the customer tries the appetizer and enjoys it, he or she may choose to order it as their entrée next time."

You will be quite surprised how well your employees will be able to take the promotion to the next level when they fully understand the *why* factor . . . Subsequently, providing customers with more information about a promotion will put them at ease, entice them, and give them an enjoyable experience.

So avoid misaligning your internal and external messages, which can cause disconnect. However, if you've already experienced miscommunication in this area, it can be remedied; let's refer back to the assessment process.

When performing the assessment be sure to include the following questions.

For consistency, we will continue using Charlie's Floral Shop.

14. What is Charlie's Floral Shop's slogan?

_____

_____

_____

15. Please share three ad campaigns you remember that were offered to the customer in the past year and include the details of the offer.

_____

_____

_____

16. Please tell us the best offer you feel Charlie's Floral Shop provided customers, and if it was well received. Please explain why or why not.

_____

_____

_____

17. Tell us what promotional offer was best received and appreciated by our customers and why.

_____

_____

_____

18. Tell us a promotional offer(s) that customers did not like and what you felt the reasons were.

_____

_____

_____

19. Please share any suggestions you have on how to make our advertising better or any idea you may have for a promotional offer.

_____

_____

_____

20. Please share any suggestions our customers have made on how to make our advertising better or any idea(s) they may have shared for a promotional offer.

_____

_____

_____

Question Fourteen: *What is Charlie's Floral Shop's slogan?*

A variety of businesses use slogans, so it's important to create one that is short and easy to remember; this will quickly help both customers and employees identify with the brand. Some companies have had the same slogan since their inception, while others may make changes if they revamp their brand.

When used properly, a slogan gives any business an automatic boost in the minds of consumers who may be shopping with that company. Here are two examples: think about "Wheaties ... The Breakfast of Champions," and "Allstate ... You're In Good Hands."

Let's look at Wheaties. Everyone knows the importance of having a good breakfast in the morning, and we all like to be winners in our daily life. The Wheaties slogan immediately presents itself as the best breakfast choice. Similarly, with the Allstate slogan, no one wants to think about a car accident or damage to his or her home, but when it happens, it's comforting to know that the insurance company of choice is going to take good care of the customer. Allstate's slogan provides that customer with confidence and assurance that Allstate will fully handle the situation.

These types of slogans help position companies apart from their competitors and leave positive thoughts in the minds of their customers. So if you have a slogan, make sure it is no more than seven words and that the message identifies with your brand. Try to avoid the typical business clichés in your slogan like offering low prices and great service; customers assume that every business will provide that. If your company does not have a slogan, research the competition to see what already exists; then conduct internal focus groups with appropriate staff members.

Whether your slogan is newly created or revised, find out if the interviewees can tell you what it is; if they cannot, disconnect exists. To avoid disconnect, the slogan must be consistently communicated across ALL advertising channels. For example, an advertiser creates a newspaper ad; it should provide the same message as the radio and billboard ad. When the ad is inconsistent, it sends a confusing message to the consumer and does not support a strong business identity. When this happens, significant advertising dollars are wasted. The point here is to keep your message, simple, concise, and consistent.

Question Fifteen: *Please share three ad campaigns you remember that were offered*

to the customer in the past year and include the details of the offer.

Most businesses run various types of promotions throughout the year. In fact, some businesses offer new promotions weekly, so asking for only three should not be an issue. The purpose of this question is to find out through the eyes of your employees, how effective your advertising is. Do your employees take time to learn about the promotions? Do your employees understand the purpose of the promotions, and do they clearly communicate it to customers? On the other hand, if your business does not do any promotional advertising, this question should not be included in your assessment.

Question Sixteen: *Please tell us the best offer you feel Charlie's Floral Shop provided customers, and if it was well received. Please explain why or why not.*

Again, for those businesses that do not provide any promotional advertising, please do not include this question in your assessment. If you are using this question, keep in mind that it is acceptable if the interviewee uses one of the promotions he or she cited in question fifteen; this reveals the promotion was well received. Explore this question with interviewees; discover what they liked about it, why they felt it was positive, and what, if anything, they believe could have made it even better.

During interviews with front-line employees, I have heard that they thought a particular promotional offer was fantastic, but the customer had a different opinion. Your employees provide that important piece . . . the "why" factor. For example, a store promoted a "BOGO" (buy one get one) offer, and when the customer arrived, he or she found out that the "BOGO" could not be combined with a 20% off coupon. This is easy to correct; in the future, simply change the store window sign or add a disclaimer so the advertising copy reads: "Coupons not applicable on "BOGO" offers."

Question Seventeen: *Tell us what promotional offer was best received and appreciated by our customers and why.*

This question may initially sound like question sixteen; however, asking this question will help you discover what promotional offer(s) your customers may have loved even if it was not financially successful. This is important to find out because a promotion may have been cancelled after it was deemed to be unsuccessful, but if it was a promotion that really appealed to your customers, perhaps reevaluating and modifying that promotion could then make it successful.

Maybe your customers came in droves, but rather than making money on the promotion, you either lost money or made much less in profits than expected. You want customers to be enticed by the promotion, but you also need it to be profitable for the business. By speaking with your employees, they should be able to share with you what attracted customers to the promotion. Perhaps it was the service discount, free warranty offer or something else that led them to respond. Then determine what you can do to make the promotion financially successful. For example, if the promotion provided a service discount, maybe the promotion can continue in the future since customers welcomed it, but with a smaller percentage off the cost.

Question Eighteen: *Tell us a promotional offer(s) that customers did not like and what you felt the reasons were.*

This question is another fact-finding mission to reveal if you are creating promotional offers that do not appeal to customers. During the interview, you may learn that customers loved the promotion, but they were not happy with the quality of the selections provided. Or, maybe you'll find that customers were not happy with the promotion because there were exclusions to it, such as a 25% off coupon did not apply, or perhaps the 50% off sale only applied to select items. Whatever the reason(s), use this opportunity to learn useful information from your employees, since they have a direct link to customers. In order to keep customers satisfied, you may have to make minor adjustments to the promotion.

Question Nineteen: *Please share any suggestions you have on how to make our*

advertising better or any idea you may have for a promotional offer.

The interviewee may or may not have answered this question as part of the earlier questions you have asked. If the question has been answered, review the suggestions that have been made. Employees are great sources for finding fresh, new ideas, which may have otherwise been overlooked. Remember it does not matter if you agree with your employees' ideas, just be sure to keep these suggestions on file for future reference. Ideas you receive now may be useful later.

Question Twenty: *Please share any suggestions our customers have made on how to make our advertising better or any idea(s) they may have shared for a promotional offer.*

The answer to this question may have already been discovered during the discussion process. Customers are always making suggestions, and hearing them from your employees gives you insight as to what your customers are thinking. Take your customers' comments seriously and you will have a vast pool of resources to draw from. It does not mean you need to incorporate every suggestion you receive, but be open to the ones that you know will improve sales and profits, as well as lead to The *Ultimate* Customer Experience.

Chapter Four

Things Don't Sell Themselves

*91% of unhappy customers will not willingly do
business with your organization again.
Source: Lee Resource Inc.*

As technology has progressed through the years, today's customer has access to information regarding any product he or she wishes to purchase. I have had many conversations with high level executives who honestly feel that because of the Internet, the customer already knows what he or she is going to purchase before going to a store, ordering online or by phone. But do products *really* sell themselves? Where did this misconception come from?

Can we assume that *every* customer already has his or her mind made up and will never ask any questions? Of course not; obviously, this type of thinking is shortsighted. Customers will have questions; imagine how they feel when there is no one available in the store to assist them and address their needs. Or what if a customer is dining at a restaurant and finds out that the server does not know what ingredients are in that "special dish?" Why do situations like these occur? The answer to the question is disconnect, along with the misconception that customers already know what they want before they make a purchase, or patronize a restaurant.

Let's talk about an experience I recently had while visiting a rather large retail consumer electronics chain. I needed a new pair of high quality headphones for my home recording studio and I was hurrying to finish a project, so I went to the nearest store in my area.

When I walked in, I found the department where the headphones were located and I was appalled at the display area. Most consumer electronics stores have useful displays set up so customers can listen to various headphones and easily go back and forth from one set to another. However, this store provided no means of letting the customer listen to the headphones. There was a rack set up with five models on display ranging from $99 to $299, yet the only way to listen was to plug the headphones directly into a Smartphone. Hopefully, any customer shopping at this store was able to get music on his or her phone. In addition, the customer could not comfortably put the headphones on because they were so close to the rack, which provided no slack to the wire. I actually had to bend down to keep them on my head. Does this make any sense? Does using these display techniques help the customer make a purchase?

Luckily for them, I knew that almost any pair of headphones would be fine for my immediate needs, but I certainly would have preferred making a purchase for all my future home studio work. I made my selection based strictly on brand name and was ready to purchase the headphones. However, I needed a store associate to get the headphones for me because all of the display boxes were not only locked onto the rack, they were also empty. Furthermore, I had already been in the store for at least fifteen minutes; no one greeted me, no one acknowledged me, and I wondered if anyone even cared that I was in the store.

I walked to the register and had to interrupt the store associate, who was having a personal conversation with another employee. I told her I wanted to purchase a pair of headphones and needed some help. She told me she would be there shortly, but did not assist me until she finished her personal conversation. At this point, I was frustrated and wanted to leave the store, but I couldn't because I knew there were no other electronics stores in the area.

Finally, the store associate came over to assist me and I told her which pair I wanted to purchase, but asked her if she had any recommendations perhaps about a different model or brand. With a puzzled look on her face, her response was simply,

"Nope, ah those are fine."

Surprisingly, the store associate did not even know that she had to go to the back room to get the headphones. While waiting for the associate to return, I tried to figure out what the difference was between the model I was purchasing and another quality brand model that was selling for $50 less. The more expensive model appeared to have a greater range of frequency, so I decided to stay with the item I was going to purchase. A few minutes later the store associate returned, and I followed her to the register. I could not resist asking her to explain the difference in products, because now I was very curious as to what type of answer I would receive. First, I inquired about the ineffective headphone display and demonstration set up. I said,

> "Please forgive me, but do customers complain about how difficult your display is to sample the headphones?"

The store associate replied,

> "That's the main office, they decide on what they want. I'm just here to ring up the purchase."

That answer really blew me away, but not as much as her answer to my next question.

> "Well, before I buy these headphones, can you please tell me what the difference is

between these headphones and that other model selling for $50.00 less?"

With a bewildered look on her face and no doubt having not a clue, her response was almost priceless . . .

"Well different manufacturers . . . they decide what they want to sell their items for."

Wow, I could not believe it. She had no knowledge of noise reduction, frequency, adapters, or any other product benefits. So again I ask, and this time directly to the chain I visited, is your merchandise just supposed to sell itself? Well I bought the headphones only out of desperation for the project I needed to finish, used them for the recording session that day, decided they were not quite right, and returned them. I bought a new pair at a different store when I had the time to drive a bit further. I do not see myself making any decent size purchases from the first consumer electronics store again. So how did they do? How was the customer experience, and how successful were they at building customer loyalty?

In this case, it was evident the store associate either did not receive adequate product training, or she simply did not pay attention during training. However once a full assessment is completed, we can determine if the cause was disconnect, or if it was the company's viewpoint that products sell themselves.

In my case, I did not use online research before going into the store. Therefore, I was solely relying on a capable store associate to help me, which clearly was not what took place.

In fact, according to a recent study from Synqera, by Instant.Ly, (May 2013) more than two-thirds of Americans prefer to shop in traditional, brick and mortar stores, rather than shop online using e-commerce sites. Here are the facts from that survey:

- 67% prefer to shop in a store
- 66% are more likely to shop in a store where they receive personal suggestions while shopping
- 80% are more likely to shop in a store that provides an overall customized shopping experience

I will admit there are many customers who use Internet research first and then go to the store to look at the product. Some may choose not to buy the product there, and then return home to order it online from another competitor. When that happens, I wonder if the retailer takes the time to ask why. Too often, the answer seems to be that the customer found a better price on a website. That may be true, but price is not always the issue. The customer was in your store, and was most likely ready and willing to buy right then and there. However, if the experience at the store was in some way lacking, then that customer chose to shop elsewhere. Does it not make sense to fix the in-store experience and eliminate losing customers? Employees play a key role within the in-store experience; therefore, they must be equipped with the necessary tools to do their jobs effectively. What do I mean by tools?

Tools are necessary resources used to carry out a particular function. It's the employer's responsibility to provide the employee with the tools needed to do his or her job effectively. Beyond customer engagement, front-line employees need to be well-versed in product knowledge in order to build the sale. Without the necessary tools, even the best employees will fail.

Let us begin with product training, or the lack thereof. In speaking with executives regarding the need for product training, some of them have said: "Our products change too often; we do not have enough time to train our employees; product training is too expensive," and more. Yet, the harsh reality of it all is that when there is product training and the store associates are knowledgeable about what products they are selling, they demonstrate a level of confidence that the customer automatically notices. A confident associate puts the customer at ease and they feel more secure in deciding whether or not to purchase the product.

Every business should encourage their employees to learn as much as possible about the their products or services, and some companies even mandate it. An apparel company can creatively incorporate product knowledge by asking employees to pull together outfits and share their ideas about fashion trends, so they can make excellent customer recommendations. A retailer selling consumer electronics, office products or appliances, can allow employees to engage in using the products and become skilled at operating them. A quick demonstration to the customer can help make the sale. A restaurant owner can schedule time for servers to sample dishes; servers with first-hand knowledge of the cuisine offered are the best salespeople. Lastly, a service business such as an insurance company or travel agency, can offer employees an opportunity to sample their services for a trial period. Remember, the employees who are in contact with your customers are <u>the</u> people who can provide the best customer experience.

Suppose you are already doing those things, but you are not sure if they are working. To find out more about what is actually taking place within your business regarding product training, let's refer back to the assessment tool and review the questions you need to ask your employees.

21. Do you enjoy the type of products that we sell? Please tell us why or why not.

_____

_____

_____

22. How knowledgeable are you about the products we sell? Do you know a lot about our products or not as much as you would like to know?

_____

_____

_____

23. Do you enjoy learning about the new products we feature in our store?

_____

_____

_____

24. Do you feel we provide enough, not enough, or too much product training?

_____

_____

_____

25. Do you take advantage of the product training we offer? If so, please tell us if you liked it, and if not, tell us why or what you do not like about it.

_____

_____

_____

26. Do you feel you are able to accurately present product features and benefits to our customers? If so, please tell us why, and if not, tell us why not.

_____

_____

_____

27. Are you able to answer our customers' questions about the products we sell?
Please tell us why or why not.

_____

_____

_____

28. Please share your best experience when communicating product features and benefits to the customer, which resulted in customer satisfaction along with a purchase.

_____

_____

_____

29. Please share an experience where you felt inadequate about your product knowledge and could not help the customer to their satisfaction or yours.

_____

_____

_____

30. Please share an experience, when because of your product knowledge, you were able to demonstrate and encourage a customer to buy a different or better product than what they were originally planning to purchase.

_____

_____

_____

Let us review the assessment questions in detail.

Question Twenty-One*: Do you enjoy the type of products that we sell? Please tell us why or why not.*

When employees truly believe in the products they sell, their passion will be conveyed to customers. For example, walk into a bookstore and talk to a store associate about a book; you can immediately notice his or her enthusiasm, which is a huge benefit to the customer experience. However, if an employee does not enjoy the products he or she is selling, consider whether that person is right for the job. If you find you have several employees who are not interested in the products you sell, then you seriously need to reconsider whom you are hiring. Their lack of enthusiasm will clearly make a negative impression on customers, and the result will be fewer sales for your business. However, if you come across employees who work hard but are unenthusiastic about selling or engaging with customers, perhaps you can consider giving them positions elsewhere in the company, unrelated to sales.

Question Twenty-Two*: How knowledgeable are you about the products we sell? Do you know a lot about our products or not as much as you would like to know*?

Employees who interact with customers are the ones who will make or break the sale and ultimately ... the customer experience. If employees feel confident and well informed about the products they sell, ask why. It may be a direct result of the product training you provide, training from a previous job, or possibly the individual has been self-taught due to his or her own personal interest.

On the other hand, if the interviewee answers that he or she does not feel knowledgeable about your products or services, find out why. As we discussed, it may be due to inadequate product training, or simply a lack of interest in the products. If the interviewee responds that he or she wants to learn more about the products or services you offer, this is a direct request asking you for additional training. Employees who excel at their jobs want to be better informed about your products, so they can engage with your customers. Customers rely on the salesperson's assistance and expertise, so make sure your employees are getting the comprehensive training they need.

Question Twenty-Three: *Do you enjoy learning about the new products we feature in our store?*

Learning about new products or services is essential to the success of your business.

Encourage employees to share detailed reasons why they may or may not enjoy this type of training, rather than only answering "yes" or "no." If several employees respond, "yes" to this question, it is a good indication that you are satisfying their desires to learn about new products and services. Ask them to elaborate on their answers in order to determine if your training can be further enhanced.

On the other hand, if you receive many negative responses to this question, perhaps task completion has taken precedence over training. Although tasks are important, employees must also be given adequate training time, so be sure your schedules are balanced. Another reason employees may not enjoy learning about new products and services could be the training itself. If the training is not engaging or does not provide sufficient content, the employee will not retain what he or she is expected to learn.

Question Twenty-Four: *Do you feel we provide enough, not enough, or too much product training?*

Some companies have a tendency to over-train. If you receive responses saying there is too much product training, your trainers may be overwhelming your salespeople with a lot more information than needed. However, if you discover that you do not provide enough product training, re-evaluate what you currently have. Ask employees what areas they feel need improvement, and make revisions as soon as possible. Keep in mind that training should be clear and concise, focusing on key elements of the product. Associates need a distinct understanding of product features and benefits, so they will be well versed when engaging customers.

Question Twenty-Five: *Do you take advantage of the product training we offer? If so, please tell us if you liked it, and if not, tell us why or what you do not like about it.*

This question will assist in determining whether or not the training you are providing is being utilized, and how effective it is. Many times a company invests in training materials and front-line employees do not make proper use of them. There are a number of reasons why this can occur, including poor communication, lack of accountability, and scheduling issues.

If responses are positive, chances are employees find your training to be relevant and they are making the most of what is offered. Should they respond negatively, find out the basis for their answers. It could be that your training is unclear or overwhelming employees with too much information. Another reason may be the methodology is tiresome, especially if too much reading is involved. The more information you receive, the easier it will be to gauge whether or not the training you are investing in should be continued as is, or if modifications need to be made.

Many companies mandate product or service training. In spite of this, if an employee is not successfully retaining the information provided, it may be that the training is not engaging. If ninety-five percent of your employees enjoy your product training, it is an excellent favorability score, and your training proves effective. On the contrary, if you receive low positive scores and high negative scores, you could be wasting time and money on ineffective training.

Question Twenty-Six*: Do you feel you are able to accurately present product features and benefits to our customers? If so, please tell us why, and if not, tell us why not.*

This question allows you to evaluate how effective your front-line employees are when communicating product features and demonstrating product benefits to customers. It reveals their levels of comfort and confidence, and also provides a gauge whereby you can measure the value of your product training. If the interviewee responds positively, inquire as to how they gained their expertise. Find out if this was directly related to your training, or if there were other factors involved. If the interviewee commented that the training was not helpful, inquire as to what areas were lacking and what improvements could be made.

As we have mentioned in previous questions, employees may have spent their own personal time learning about your products, so do not make any assumptions that your training was responsible for their expertise. On the other hand, if trainees respond that their skills were acquired directly from your training, ask them to share how it has helped them perform their jobs more effectively.

This information will guide you in evaluating both the positive and negative aspects of your training.

Question Twenty-Seven: *Are you able to answer our customers' questions about the products we sell? Please tell us why or why not.*

While it is extremely important for employees to possess product or service knowledge, it is equally as important for them to know how to listen to customers' needs and answer their questions correctly. Simply knowing details about a product or service is not enough; a successful salesperson will also understand why that product or service is right for the customer.

For example, a top furniture salesperson does an excellent job describing to a customer the construction, durability and finance options available on a dining room set. However, if the customer has questions regarding how the furniture will fit in his or her dining area, or blend in with the wall color, the salesperson must be equipped to respond to those concerns as well. If the salesperson does not listen attentively and answer the customer's questions accurately, the risk of losing the sale is high.

Question Twenty-Eight: *Please share your best experience when communicating product features and benefits to the customer, which*

resulted in customer satisfaction along with a purchase.

Unless you are talking to an employee on his or her first day of employment, every employee involved in selling should be able to easily answer this question. If the employee answers positively, listen to the story and ask if you can share it with other employees. Story sharing is an outstanding motivational tool and provides recognition to the employee who had the experience.

If the employee cannot think of any positive experiences, again consider if this person is right for the job. You cannot afford to employ representatives who are unable to effectively interact with customers. When this happens, sales are lost, which will have a tremendously negative impact on your business.

Question Twenty-Nine: Please share an experience where you felt inadequate about your product knowledge and could not help the customer to their satisfaction or yours.

Every employee, no matter how talented, knowledgeable, or experienced, has probably encountered this problem at some time in his or her career. The experience for the employee can be quite painful. For example, suppose a new product or service was introduced, but it was not accompanied by product or service training, or the information provided was incorrect or outdated. This could have a major impact on your salespeople. Another reason may be that your business did not have the right product or service to meet the customer's need. In that case, no matter what the salesperson offered, it just did not work for the customer. The point here is that employees who interact with customers must receive all the tools necessary for competent job performance.

> **Question Thirty:** *Please share an experience, when because of your product knowledge, you were able to demonstrate and encourage a customer to buy a different or better product than what they were originally planning to purchase.*

Here is an opportunity to evaluate how well the selling process is working for the company. When employees make accurate recommendations, the customer experience will be taken to a new level. Winning a customer's trust is beneficial for repeat business. Furthermore, customers will tell their family and friends that your business had the capability to supply them with what they really needed, and not what they thought they wanted.

In summary, products and services do <u>not</u> sell themselves. When employees are well trained, knowledgeable, courteous and helpful to customers, they have a much greater opportunity to make a sale and most importantly, build The *Ultimate* Customer Experience.

You have now completed the first part of this book and are ready to conduct the full assessment. Create a list of employees you will interview and decide who will conduct the interviews. You must write down all the answers received, and if desired, you can record them and refer back later if you wish to double check an answer, comment, or share a story. Once you have conducted all the interviews, move on to the next chapter, which will discuss the assessment report and action plan.

The following page has all the questions we have discussed. For consistency, we are using Charlie's Floral shop throughout the assessment. Copy the questions and modify them in accordance with the needs of your business.

ASSESSMENT REVIEW FORM

Name: _____

Title: _____

Length of time and experience with Charlie's Floral Shop: _____

The above information will be kept confidential when reporting survey results.

1. Describe the company vision as delivered by the leaders of the company.

_____
_____
_____

2. What do you feel are the important short-term and long-term goals for Charlie's Floral Shop?

_____

_____

_____

3. When you hear "Charlie's Floral Shop," what image comes to mind?

_____

_____

_____

4. How would your customers describe Charlie's Floral Shop?

_____

_____

_____

5. On a scale of 1-10 (10 being the highest) how would you rate customer service, such as greeting and engaging the customer, and assisting the customer?

_____

_____

_____

6. On a scale of 1-10 (10 being the highest) how would you rate your business regarding inviting the customer back?

_____

_____

_____

7. How long have you been working for Charlie's Floral Shop?

_____

_____

_____

8. Do you like your job? If "Yes," tell us why and if "No" please elaborate on the reasons.

_____

_____

_____

9. Do you feel you are appreciated and recognized for your contribution to the company?

_____

_____

_____

10. Do you like your customers? If so, why and if not, please elaborate.

_____

_____

_____

11. Tell us your best experience in satisfying a customer.

_____

_____

_____

12. Tell us the worst experience you had with a customer.

_____

_____

_____

13. How do you handle getting your tasks done and assisting customers? Explain what you do.

_____

_____

_____

14. What is Charlie's Floral Shop's slogan?

_____

_____

_____

15. Please share three ad campaigns you remember, that were offered to the customer in the past year and include the details of the offer.

_____

_____

_____

16. Please tell us the best offer you feel Charlie's Floral Shop provided customers, and if it was well received. Please explain why or why not.

_____

_____

_____

17. Tell us what promotional offer was best received and appreciated by our customers and why.

_____

_____

_____

18. Tell us a promotional offer(s) that customers did not like and what you felt the reasons were.

_____

_____

_____

19. Please share any suggestions you have on how to make our advertising better or any idea you may have for a promotional offer.

_____

_____

_____

20. Please share any suggestions our customers have made on how to make our advertising better or any idea(s) they may have shared for a promotional offer.

_____

_____

_____

21. Do you enjoy the type of products that we sell? Please tell us why or why not.

_____

_____

_____

22. How knowledgeable are you about the products we sell? Do you know a lot about our products or not as much as you would like to know?

_____

_____

_____

23. Do you enjoy learning about the new products we feature in our store?

_____

_____

_____

24. Do you feel we provide enough, not enough, or too much product training?

_____

_____

_____

25. Do you take advantage of the product training we offer? If so, please tell us if you liked it, and if not, tell us why or what you do not like about it.

_____

_____

_____

26. Do you feel you are able to accurately present product features and benefits to our customers? If so, please tell us why, and if not, tell us why not.

_____

_____

_____

27. Do you feel you are able to answer our customers' questions about the products we sell?
Please tell us why or why not.

_____

_____

_____

28. Please share your best experience when communicating product features and benefits to the customer, which resulted in customer satisfaction along with a purchase.

_____

_____

_____

29. Please share an experience where you felt inadequate about your product knowledge and could not help the customer to their satisfaction or yours.

_____

_____

_____

30. Please share an experience, when because of your product knowledge, you were able to demonstrate and encourage a customer to buy a different or better product than what they were originally planning to purchase.

_____

_____

_____

Chapter Five

Quick Fix Solutions Do Not Work . . . Action Plans Do!

A dissatisfied consumer will tell between 9 and 15 people about their experience. About 13% of dissatisfied customers tell more than 20 people. Source: White House Office of Consumer Affairs, Washington, DC

I will never forget an experience I had years ago while at my first business. Across from my office was a well-known supermarket chain. I would frequently shop there to pick up items for the office and whenever I did, the slow service at the registers always bothered me. The lines were usually ten or more customers long, and it was quite frustrating when I only had a few items and the express lanes were just as long.

One day, upon arriving at the store, I noticed signs everywhere that said . . .

"No More Than Three!" Under the big headline was smaller print that further explained what this meant—if at any time there were more than three people waiting at the register, the store would immediately open another register.

I walked through the supermarket and picked up the various items I needed. I was actually looking forward to checking out and experiencing the new program for myself. Knowing the store well, it would not be long before at least one register would have more than three, if not eight people waiting on line. When I arrived at the registers, I could not believe my eyes. The signs stating "No More Than Three" were hanging from the ceiling right in front of the registers, yet at no time did I see a line with fewer than five people. As usual, only four out of twelve register stations were open.

A store employee was walking by, and I asked him politely why there were signs everywhere promoting shorter lines, but the lines were still long. I could not believe his answer:

"It's a new program they started. But it can't work here."

Then he just walked away. I went back to the store two days later and experienced the same situation: long lines, while the "No More Than Three" signs hung in front of the registers. I asked another employee about it and she answered,

"Oh, it's a program the main office started."

When I asked her why were there still long lines, she said,

"Oh, I don't think everyone is familiar with it yet."

Then she walked away. I still could not believe these answers.

This actually continued for three months. As I continued to inquire, one assistant manager told me the problem was a staff shortage, and the corporate office would not allow him additional payroll dollars to hire more cashiers. He said he felt the program was a great idea, but not practical because he did not have enough staff to support it.

Finally, during the last week the signs were up, I spoke with a different store manager who was new to the location. When I mentioned a shortage in payroll dollars, she gave a different explanation and told me that the former manager did an inadequate job of scheduling his people. This store manager must have been right because she had the signs removed the following week, and within two weeks of her taking over, the long register lines disappeared. Due to her ability as a manager, she was able to schedule her employees properly and made sure that there were always enough registers open.

The point made here is that although the corporate office of this chain developed a program for reducing register lines, the program on its own could not fix the problem. In speaking with the new store manager, she did admit to me that long lines were a problem not just in the store where I shopped, but also in many of the chain's other locations. In essence, the quick fix "No More Than Three" program did not work. Companies that rely on "quick-fix" solutions will not reach the level of success they are aiming for.

So how do you develop an effective action plan that will implement the right culture, and eliminate disconnect within your business? First, do not make the mistake many top-level executives do after visiting some of their locations. These executives come in energized on a Monday morning with an instant plan, determined to solve the problem they've discovered.

If you take this approach to solve your disconnect, all you will end up with is another "No More Than Three" failed program. I have also seen many situations where high-level executives spend days in meetings with what they believe will be the finest program, filled with enthusiasm, concepts and plans. They get their training people involved and assign them the mission of developing and implementing the program. Months go by before the program is delivered, and when it finally is, the interest and support in the program is long gone. What the company is left with is nothing more than another failed program and more wasted dollars.

Let's assume you have performed your assessment as outlined in the previous chapters. If so, use the assessment as your guide when coming up with your action plan. Build this plan with permanent solutions that will achieve your goals, not short-term fixes that lead to failure. As you assemble your plan, proceed carefully and take one step at a time.

Through the assessment, you have taken the first substantial step in learning the needs of your business. Go back and look at the information you gathered and remember to organize it so it can be easily utilized. Use percentages in order to quickly determine results. Let's use the first question as an example; the question was: "Describe the company vision as delivered by the leaders of the company."

You should know the answer. Begin by counting the responses you received, and align those responses with the correct answer (or as close to the appropriate answers that you are willing to accept) in one group and the remaining answers in another group. If you had 50 respondents and 40 knew the answer, then you can say 80% responded with the correct answer and 20% did not. It does not matter if you received answers that did not state the exact verbiage set up by your corporate office (unless this is something you previously stipulated). As long as the interviewees had the appropriate concept and an overall understanding of your company vision, their answers should be acceptable.

Repeat this process for every question you asked. Organize the information by first identifying the question with the questionnaire number. Document your percentage results and include each question's comments or suggestions. Once you have completed this process, take time to read your results and then share them with appropriate team members. The next step is creating an action plan that will be effective, and not just result in a "quick fix" approach. The action plan must provide the solutions for eliminating any disconnect your assessment has found, as well as implement the right culture—one that will last and become an everyday part of your business.

As you are analyzing your results, list all issues that need resolution. It is acceptable if every answer shows the need for improvement. Rank the improvements needed by priority. For example, in reviewing results, if you see that only 10% of your employees are not familiar with your promotions, but 70% feel they need more product training, then rank product training higher in priority. Do this for the entire assessment and soon you will have what you need to put together a strong action plan. The action plan will be divided in two parts: "Short-Term Needs" and "Long-Term Needs."

With each question, review the responses and see how they relate to your company's vision. For example, remember Charlie's Floral Shop's vision: "To become the leading Mid-Western floral chain known for outstanding customer service and satisfaction."

In Charlie's assessment, suppose it revealed that his employees answered question eleven unsatisfactorily, which was, "Tell us your best experience in satisfying a customer." How could

Charlie ever achieve his goal of being known for outstanding customer service and satisfaction, when his employees do not understand his vision of service?

If this problem existed, it would be vital for the success of Charlie's Floral Shop to completely revamp its culture, so that every employee will clearly understand his or her role regarding Charlie's customer service expectations. Charlie's Floral Shop would need to re-train its employees on a variety of issues in order to fix this problem and this would not be a one-time training session. Ultimately, it is Charlie's responsibility to provide all the necessary tools to achieve these expectations.

Without taking this approach, there would be absolutely no way Charlie would ever come close to achieving the vision he has for his stores, regardless of what merchandise he sells or what prices he offers. He may still have a successful business, but never the business he is aspiring to have.

As you review your assessment responses, organize them and develop an effective tool whereby you utilize percentages of pros and cons from every response, along with any pieces of valuable information obtained during the interview process. Make a list of what areas you are pleased with and put them in a separate group. This information will be helpful because in some cases, you may be able to expand what has been successful in a particular area or duplicate it for another area. For example, suppose you find that overall your employees feel appreciated and recognized. If so, that is a tremendous benefit and goes a long way in providing The *Ultimate* Customer Experience.

Perhaps you find out that the reason your employees feel appreciated is because you provide special compensation when they achieve certain goals, such as a free lunch, or maybe a contest offering a chance to win a free trip. If that is the case, you can see that your employees enjoy these incentives and you may wish to use the same means to achieve goals in other areas that need improvement. The more you learn from the results of your assessment, the easier it will be to achieve your goals.

When reviewing the responses, be fair with what you have received. Do not attack, reprimand or dismiss employees simply because they do not satisfy you with their responses—unless they are insubordinate. Remember, it begins with you. Think of the questions you asked and what you would have answered if someone were interviewing you, and be honest with yourself. I stated earlier that providing the best customer experience starts with the person at the top, and in no way could the environment ever be, "Do as I say, and not as I do." If you would like your employees to treat customers and each other courteously, make sure you are demonstrating the same behavior.

In Chapter Two, we spoke about developing the right culture for your business. Moreover, we discussed how that must come from you, as the company's leader. As you look through the questions and read the responses, are you happy with them or are you disappointed? In all probability, it will be a mixture of both.

Developing and implementing an action plan based on the information obtained from your assessment can accomplish what is necessary, regardless of how much improvement is needed. However, stop for a moment and take a good look at yourself as a leader. Judging by the assessment responses, how are you seeing yourself and your company? If your employees are pleased working for you, then you are off to an excellent start. If not, changes need to be made. To elaborate further, read the following short story about an entrepreneur who did not understand how to maximize his employees' efforts. Here's the story:

I was once providing marketing services for a small home theatre business. The company's advanced technology and knowledgeable staff positioned them significantly ahead of their competition. However, the owner of the company had the worst people skills I had ever seen. He would constantly berate his employees, and there was never a "thank you" or a "please" when he spoke to them. Every meeting he had with his staff was full of criticisms, which certainly did not make his staff feel like they were part of the team or appreciated. For example, if he felt someone did not charge enough for a particular service, he would say things like "I am losing money," or, "I don't care what you think, it's <u>my</u> company."

Perhaps the employee didn't charge enough for the service; if so, simply say, "I know you meant well, but next time we'll need to charge more money because our profit margin on this job was too low." That type of response certainly sounds much more pleasant and helps the employee understand what is expected and what action needs to be taken on his or her part to improve. Company goals will never be achieved if employees feel reprimanded for trying to do their best. The owner of the home theatre company and I formed a working relationship. Upon several occasions, I shared with him that he should not speak to his employees in such a harsh manner, and they would be more receptive if he changed his tactics. The company was too small to hire me to perform an assessment, but I tried to use my experience by letting him know that he was destroying his own business with his lack of communication skills. Unfortunately, he did not listen. My time with his company was short, lasting only about three months; I could no longer work with him because he was the most ungrateful employer I had ever met.

A year later, I ran into one of his employees who had left the company.

The former employee told me that their business environment only grew worse and the owner went so far as to try to cheat his salespeople out of their commissions. The owner would call customers to confirm that the price quotes they received were the same as what was shown on the sales representatives' documentation, fearing that his salespeople were cheating him. Eventually, all of his top employees quit and shortly after, the company went bankrupt. Therefore, what did this employer gain with his attitude? Nothing—and he lost his business because of it. So, take the assessment process seriously. Carefully review the questions and responses and record all areas that need improvement.

If you find employees are speaking favorably through their responses regarding working for you, that is exceptional. If that's not the case, figure out through the information you have received how you can change your business environment and culture. Review your assessment responses carefully and be honest with yourself about how you and your management team treat your employees.

Providing excellent customer service starts at the top, meaning it starts with you. Be courteous and kind to your employees, and they will treat your customers in the same manner. You are the leader, the one they will look up to and follow. Always put yourself in the other person's shoes. Let's explore how putting together an action plan will improve employee communication and recognition.

The goal is to improve your culture and eliminate disconnect within your business. Think about the assessment responses you received, particularly to questions asking if the employee likes his or her job. These questions will reveal many details about how employees feel working for your company. As the leader of your business, it is important that you and your management team show employees they are appreciated.

As you develop your action plan, strive to improve both employee communication and recognition. Include a positive approach for speaking with employees, and be sure that your management team is in agreement. Praise your employees when they do well, and thank them for their hard work. If you were the employee, wouldn't you appreciate that? Nevertheless, if you or your managers must correct an employee about something that was done wrong, begin with an encouraging comment, and then use connecting words like, "however" or "but." No one wants to hear bad news, but if the employee is also recognized for his or her exemplary work, he or she will accept the correction much better and will be eager to resolve the problem.

Accept the fact that everyone makes mistakes. Your employees will make them, and you will too. Remember this point when correcting or reprimanding an employee; ineffective communication will only lead to more mistakes. Also, remember that customers understand mistakes will happen.

However, what matters most is how the employee handles the situation. Do they go out of their way to correct the problem, or do they sweep it under the carpet? Review the responses particularly relating to how well your employees feel they satisfy customers' needs. Look closely at questions that relate to providing a positive customer experience, either by solving a problem or by up-selling the client to a better product. These responses will provide an indication of how well your company is doing regarding customer satisfaction, as well as employee communication.

The following example demonstrates how a company handled a situation with an employee that could have resulted in lost business. As you read the story, put yourself in the manager's position to see how you would have handled it. Moreover, think about your responses and see if any of them stand out in showing the need for managers to better deal with subordinates when they make mistakes.

A few years ago, I was traveling with one of my employees, so I reserved two rooms for two nights at an upscale hotel. Upon arriving at the hotel, the front desk agent greeted us and asked me if I had received her message. My answer was "no," and to my knowledge there was no message. The agent proceeded to tell me that the hotel was completely full, so she needed to change my two rooms, which were single one-bedroom suites, into one two-bedroom suite. There was no, "may we do this?" or, "would it be all right if we did this?" Instead, she already made the change. My employee and I were exhausted after traveling all day and we had no choice but to accept the new reservation.

I wanted to see how the corporate office would respond to this situation, so once in my room, I called their toll-free number. Within minutes, I was speaking to a representative who transferred me to someone higher up in the company, who then transferred me to someone even higher. The hotel's efforts to correct the problem pleased me, and I realized that the corporate office did care about my business and was doing everything they could to accommodate me. First, they attempted to find two rooms in their nearby hotels, but they did not have any available close enough to the hotel I was already in. So unfortunately, the hotel I was in was still the best choice. The call with the corporate office ended positively, and the person I was speaking with agreed that the situation was unacceptable and said a hotel manager would call me shortly.

Although it was the manager's day off, the hotel representative assured me that the manager would be contacted and he would call me directly. I agreed, hung up, and waited.

Upon speaking with the manager, he first made the mistake of defending the employee. Within a few minutes of hearing my position, he apologized but explained that there were no other rooms in the hotel. We would have to either stay in the two-bedroom suite, or we could check out and go somewhere else. I was now more furious than ever, but it was late so I ended the call and went into my bedroom saying to myself, "Time for a hotel chain change."

What I did not know was that apparently the corporate office followed up with the manager after my call. The next morning at breakfast, the manager greeted us and was quite apologetic and accommodating. After he finished apologizing for at least ten minutes, he said that after we spoke, he called his boss at the main office to get permission for the accommodations he wanted to give me. This was the manager's way of making amends. By the time he was through speaking with us, we received two separate suites for our second night, no charge for both nights, and an additional 10,000 points on my membership club card. The manager went on to say that the employee who changed the reservation was new and that this never should have happened. He could not stop apologizing.

I immediately saw his sincerity and thanked him for how he handled the situation. As we finished breakfast and walked back to our room, I overheard him speaking with the employee. He said,

"Do you see that man? That's Mr. Suriano and he's the guest whose reservation you changed last night. Mr. Suriano is an important hotel guest. I understand that we were overbooked last night and why you thought what you did would solve the problem. Nonetheless, you can NEVER change anyone's reservation, no matter what the circumstances. You can however, when absolutely necessary, ask a guest if you can change his or her reservation, which is what you attempted to do—but you have to speak to the guest directly, not just leave a message. The message you left Mr. Suriano was never heard because he was traveling all day."

The employee listened carefully as the manager explained not only what she did wrong, but also *why* it was wrong. Then he asked her the most important question:

"Now that I have explained this, do you understand what you did wrong and do you understand that you can never do it again?"

The employee said yes and the manager asked her to explain everything back to him. She did it perfectly, which proved she understood her error and why she could never do it again. It was an effective criticism of her mistake and a fair reprimand. The manager did not scold or chastise the employee.

This experience demonstrates the manager's equitable approach, which helped the employee understand the mistake and why it was imperative to never make that error again. I could tell the employee appreciated that the manager handled the situation without a harsh reprimand. More than anything, I was impressed with how the manager handled the situation. Other managers may have even fired the employee.

Since then, we have stayed at the hotel many more times, and each time following the request of the manager, we would call him directly when booking a reservation. From that time until he left his job at the hotel, every time we stayed there, he made sure to make time for us and always gave us some type of special accommodation. I am pleased to say that the hotel chain recognized his abilities. He did not actually leave the hotel chain, but received a promotion to a higher position.

Looking back, the experience went from frustrating to excellent because the corporate office knew how to provide The *Ultimate* Customer Experience and so did the hotel manager. Yes, the manager could have yelled at her and maybe she would have quit; worse yet, he could have fired her. As a result of how well the manager handled the situation, that same employee is still working at the hotel and apparently doing a fine job, providing excellent customer service to thousands of guests through the years. She does her job well, with pride and with the vision of the hotel chain's corporate office. Every time I visit the hotel, I am pleased to see how much that employee has grown professionally, and how well she interacts with all the guests.

Success starts at the top, and the corporate office knew how to treat its customer, as did the manager. Moreover, the manager knew how to treat the employee. It is obvious that they do not believe in "quick fix" solutions, but rather a culture that puts the customer first. Take time to review all your responses and put together a comprehensive action plan that will address the challenges and issues you wish to improve from your findings.

Chapter Six

Education vs. Information

Happy customers who get their issue resolved tell about 4 to 6 people about their experience.
Source: White House Office of Consumer Affairs, Washington, DC

A business man named Joe owned a large retail store. Once inside, customers loved the huge selection of merchandise, the service, and the fantastic prices. Joe always spent a lot of money on advertising, which attracted plenty of new customers, as well as existing ones. However, Joe had one significant problem . . . new customers always had difficulty figuring out how to enter his store. The building was old and the front door blended in with the facade of the building. Unless a customer walked out or another customer walked in, new customers could almost never find the front door.

One day out of frustration, Joe called in his assistant, Jenny, and told her to send out a memo to the proper department, requesting a solution to the problem. Jenny immediately sent out a memo that read:

This problem <u>must</u> be solved:

"How to Enter The Store"

Jenny had a very busy morning and accidentally sent the memo to the "training department." Once read, Maureen, the Training Director, immediately began to work on the issue. First, she assembled her staff for a series of meetings on how to address the problem. What should the objectives be? What should the methodology be? How will we test results? After two months of meetings, it was clear on how to proceed. The training department would develop a manual and a video so everyone would know how to enter the building. For six months, they worked diligently, listing every piece of information. Then for the next six months, a full color, 300-page manual was produced along with a 30-minute video. No topic went unnoticed.

In the manual, one could easily find:

How To Enter The Building:

- If Right-Handed
- If Left-Handed
- If Holding A Child
- If Wheeling A Stroller
- If Pregnant
- If In A Wheel Chair
- If On Crutches

Along with such topics:

- The Proper Way To Pull Open the Door
- How To Properly Shift Your Weight When Opening The Door

There were diagrams and text covering all the details of every topic. The video allowed the individual to see visual examples of what they read.

After testing the materials themselves over the next three months, the training department made 5,000 copies and hired additional staff to stand in the parking lot, to ensure that every customer who parked there received a set of instructions.

On the day the program was to be rolled out, Joe just happened to confront his assistant Jenny, arguing that it's been over 15 months and the problem is still not resolved. Just then, a very proud Maureen stopped in Joe's office and handed him a set of the new training materials entitled: "How to Enter The Store."

Joe was completely outraged. Immediately he picked up the phone and called Ed, the head of the advertising/marketing department, the one department who is trained on saying as much as they can in as few words as possible. The next day the problem was solved. While pulling into the parking lot, Joe noticed a big sign hanging over the front door. It said only one word:

<u>*"ENTRANCE"*</u>

The point of this story: many companies more often than not, over-train employees. The purpose of training is to teach employees what they need to know in order to do their jobs effectively—nothing more and nothing less. Over-training results in confusion and low retention; it is also costly, time consuming and hinders the new employee from starting off on the right foot.

Companies usually understand the need for training and spend significant dollars each year; yet, very few really know what they are getting in return for their money. As a result, even with a large investment in training, they may find out that their training can be doing more harm than good. Effective training improves business culture, as well as employee performance; it also eliminates disconnect, maintains consistency throughout the company and increases sales. These elements create a formula that successfully builds The *Ultimate* Customer Experience. Let us look at training carefully. How much is too much? What key information is needed for the success of your business?

The first step to achieving effective training begins by addressing the following three questions when developing any training module or program:

1) What key points are necessary for this training program?

2) What information does an employee need to know in order to perform his or her job correctly?

3) Beyond job skills, what does each employee need to know about the company?

Answers to those three simple questions will provide an outline needed to create effective training programs for any company. Let's look at each question individually.

1) What key points are necessary for this training program?

Suppose the mission is to create a product knowledge training program for a "digital clock radio with Wi-Fi." What are the important features and benefits the front-line employee needs to know? Keep in mind that the average customer will have questions like,

"What would I use the Wi-Fi for?"

"How easy is it to program and how many different times can I set?"

"Does it change time automatically for Daylight Savings?"

Typically, the merchandise buyer is responsible for ordering this item for the business and is the most qualified person to identify the "key" points, features and benefits for the product. Moreover, those key points should be explained in priority order.

2) What information does an employee need to know in order to perform his or her job correctly?

Look over the product features and benefits list. The employee should have a clear understanding of the product, as well as 5-7 of the top features and benefits. The front-line employee should know answers to the most common questions that customers will ask about the product. To ensure accurate product selection, the employee should be knowledgeable about the types of questions to ask the customer regarding his or her need for the product.

For example, if the customer does not have Wi-Fi, there is most likely no practical reason to recommend this product. If there is another feature that is only available on the Wi-Fi model, and that feature is one that the customer absolutely wants, then the product can still be recommended. Simply said, the training teaches the employee how to ascertain the customer's needs, how to make the right recommendations, and how to satisfy the customer overall.

3) Beyond job skills, what does each employee need to know about the company?

Every company has unique assets that differentiate them from their competitors. Identify three or four of these elements and incorporate them into every training program.

These three or four key benefits need to be part of every training program so the employee can embrace and incorporate them into his or her customer interactions. For example, if a company's main strength is customer service, then whatever is unique concerning customer service should be consistently reinforced throughout each training module. Keep the "message" of why customers should do business with you simple. The reasons why you believe your company provides exceptional customer service must be clearly defined, so that it becomes part of your culture.

Next, when developing a training module, always consider the length of time. The golden rule is that no training module should be longer than 30 minutes. After 30 minutes, the trainee begins to lose concentration, as well as the ability to absorb what is being taught. Also, avoid asking the trainee to perform the same task for the entire training period. Basically, avoid reading or video watching for 30 minutes straight. Break up the training into different presentation methods to keep the trainee engaged. For example, break up reading with a physical exercise. If video watching is mandatory, keep it short and follow it up with something creative, such as a role-play exercise. However, when more than 30 minutes is necessary for a training topic, break it up into 30 minute sections, but do not give the trainee more than one section at a time, and allow 15-minute breaks in between sections.

There seems to be a misconception shared by many trainers that in order for training to be effective and thorough, it must be presented in great length. Where trainers make this mistake, especially with new hires, is balancing what they need to learn and what the trainer wants them to learn. That's why it's imperative to begin with the three basic questions we just discussed, and incorporate them into the 30-minute training module.

The best example I can offer took place a few years ago. A large convenience store chain had an issue with coffee making procedures and hired my company to address its problem. We soon discovered that the employees who should have been making fresh coffee every two hours were often letting it sit for as long as eight hours. Furthermore, instead of using one coffee packet in their machines, many employees were using as many as four packets. You could imagine customers' reactions coming in late afternoon for a fresh Cup of Joe, only to find terrible tasting coffee.

The company's training department produced a two-hour training module, consisting of a large manual that the store manager, as well as seasoned employees, used to provide new hire training. After reviewing the materials, we found the trainer had included too much information. Using our patented training methodology, our company was able to produce a self-paced training module that was 30 minutes long and included every piece of information that was necessary—and nothing more. We were able to reduce training time by 75%, and eliminate the need for the store manager or store employee to conduct the training, which also saved the company payroll dollars. Most importantly, in fewer than 30 days from the rollout of our training, we solved their problem. The company went on to save almost one million dollars a year by eliminating coffee packet waste, and they sold more coffee because it was always fresh. The point is that we concentrated on what the store associates needed to know. As I have said repeatedly, the purpose of training is to teach people the skills they need to do their job, nothing more and nothing less. In the case of the convenience store chain, its coffee training module was too long, contained too much information, and was boring. The trainee was unable to understand the required procedures, and therefore the training was unsuccessful.

Another important item to remember when developing training is that every module should begin with the subject matter that will be covered. I am often astounded when we review the client's existing training and we find a program that begins without any mention of its purpose. The trainer who developed the module often assumes that the trainee will automatically know what material will be included. Successful training involves effective communication supported by clear instruction.

Training must be engaging and "fun" to a certain degree. When I say "fun," I do not mean ridiculous. Avoid styles that are juvenile and demeaning to trainees, such as using cartoons and characters, thinking that trainees will be amused. I am all for introductions and "icebreakers" in classroom settings, but I once watched a trainer conduct a class that played a game called "Suck and Blow." Here adults were given a straw and put into teams. The objective was to get a small paper ball back and forth from one team member to another, by blowing or inhaling through the straw to balance the paper ball. This type of "icebreaker" served no purpose to the training, wasted twenty minutes, and accomplished nothing. After the class, I asked the instructor why she played this game. Her reply was that it broke the ice with the group. What she did not know was that I also asked individuals after the class how they felt playing "Suck and Blow." Their answers ranged from feeling foolish to being embarrassed; they did not appreciate it. Buffoonery is ineffective, and trainers must remember to always respect their trainees— they are people too.

On another occasion, I was meeting with a new client and decided to visit some of their stores in order to get a sense of some issues they were having and what type of training they were providing for new hires. In speaking with the store manager, she was elated that corporate hired an outside solution provider. The manager, along with the new hires, shared their dislike of the in-house training; it proved to be ineffective, so the manager used it minimally. In fact, recently an employee was found asleep while utilizing their computer-based training. Unsuccessful computer-based training is a prominent problem amongst many businesses, and this contributes to wasted dollars.

Chapter Seven

Training . . . Know
The Essentials

*Even in a negative economy, customer experience
is a high priority for consumers, with 60% often or
always paying more for a better experience.
Source: Harris Interactive, Customer Experience
Impact Report*

Before we discuss the most important topics
new hires need to master, let's take a brief look at
how much training an employee should receive.
To answer this question, first you need a clear job
description for every position you fill.

Begin with front-line employees, whose
positions include sales associate, customer service
or account representative, restaurant server, as
well as low to mid-level management. Depending
on the position, a front-line new hire may require
twenty to thirty hours of effective training. However,
some companies mandate as many as eighty hours
of front-line new hire training. In addition, these
employees will typically need about two to four
hours of supplemental training per month to expand
their product knowledge and to inform them of any
new company developments.

If you are satisfied with the amount of training time your company supplies, as well as the topics covered for new hire training, congratulations. Your training staff should be commended. If not, continue to read on and you will soon understand why you could be creating disconnect within your company.

Below are 10 basic topics that should be included when developing a curriculum for new hires. Depending on your industry or the service you provide, you will most likely have more than 10 topics for training, but the 10 topics listed in this chapter are the most essential for any company. Keep in mind that not every one of these topics may be relevant for all businesses.

- o New Hire Orientation
- o Customer Service
- o Sales Culture Management
- o Sales Techniques
- o Operations (POS, Systems Training, RF Guns, Etc.)
- o Product Knowledge
- o Merchandising
- o Safety
- o Management Skill Development
- o HR Issues/Associate Relations

These ten topics can be modified and expanded upon to include specific information that applies to your industry. We will discuss general principles that apply to each topic. Keep in mind that I am focusing solely on front-line employees who interact primarily with the customer.

New Hire Orientation: This is <u>THE</u> most important training topic and sets the tone for the new hire; therefore, it should be the first module a new hire participates in. The New Hire Orientation module must address employee responsibilities and what it means to be a team member. Be clear about company expectations and explain why they are synonymous with customer expectations. However, when discussing company policy, be sure it's not conveyed as one long list of Do's and Do Not's. The New Hire Orientation module must include your company vision, culture, policies and procedures, as well as any unique differences that separate your company from competitors. It is imperative that new hires understand why their contribution to your business is significant. If you truly wish to provide the *Ultimate* Customer Experience, begin with New Hire Orientation and explain that there is no one, or nothing, more important than the customer. Continue that theme throughout ALL of your training.

Customer Service: The purpose of customer service training is to educate employees on your customer service objectives, company philosophy, and why the customer is essential to the success of your business. Instruction on this topic is not a one-time event; therefore, it cannot be covered in one module. Incorporate the key elements of this module into all other training programs; this will plant a seed and build a foundation for providing the *Ultimate* Customer Experience.

Many businesses do not have an established customer service program; if your business does not have one in place, strongly consider creating one. If budget is an issue, there are many generic programs out there that you can use as a guide, but at some point it is imperative to create a "custom" program that is suitable for your business.

A common mistake made by trainers is that they often attempt to put every aspect of customers' needs into one program and then call it customer service. It is fine to have a module entitled "Customer Service" if it explains the customer service program, the different steps, and most importantly, explains the "Why" factor for each step. In order for customer service to become embedded in the business culture, the key initiatives of customer service must be present in every training module, no matter what the topic of that module is. Front-line employees deal with your customers on a regular basis; you can only omit customer service initiatives when employees are trained on topics where the customer is never present, such as "Stockroom Inventory."

Customer service begins with a proper greeting. If the customer service training is designed for retail, customers should be greeted within 30 seconds or less. If it is for a restaurant, patrons should be greeted immediately. And, if customers are contacting you primarily by phone, make sure the recorded messages are friendly and customized for your business. Be sure the representative taking the call repeats your message to the customer and maintains the friendly tone that was conveyed on the recording. Customers contacting you by phone should be greeted in the same manner as if you were speaking to them in person.

Trainees need to understand the importance of smiling and establishing a pleasant rapport with the customer. They must also learn how to engage the customer by asking the right questions, listening closely, and properly responding to the customer's questions. Unfortunately, fear of customers often hinders the trainee's ability to participate in customer engagement. When customer service training does not teach trainees how to engage the customer, trainees fear the customer might ask a question they do not have an answer to, so they simply avoid the customer altogether. To eliminate this issue, create easy to use open-ended questions, as well as supportive dialogue.

In order to break the ice, teach employees to discuss topics unrelated to business, such as the weather, a sporting event, or some other subject that they are comfortable with. Opening a dialogue with these types of topics is often the start of a very successful "sales" conversation. Nevertheless, explain to employees that they do not need to bombard customers with unnecessary questions. Your customer service program should also include role-playing with another associate, so the trainee can become more comfortable making conversation with customers.

Additionally, employees avoid customer engagement when customer service training has not impressed upon them the concept that there is no one, or nothing, more important than the customer. The absence of this concept is often seen when employees struggle to balance task completion with customer service responsibilities. For example, managers frequently pile on tasks and insist their employees complete them promptly. When this happens, store associates are afraid to break away momentarily from their tasks to assist the customer, for fear of being reprimanded by a manager later on. Of course, tasks are important and need to be completed in a timely fashion, but not at the customers' expense.

Sales Culture Management: This topic is often categorized incorrectly and viewed as an element of customer service. Technically, it is not. By sales culture, I am referring to the approach you wish your sales associates to take. Some businesses do not believe in implementing aggressive sales practices, and instead prefer a soft sell approach, while others prefer the sales associates to be very persistent; the choice is yours. This program defines your company's sales philosophy, teaches the trainees how to embrace it, and succeed with it. Include in this training program the unique dynamics of your business—for example, do you have a private label credit card? If so, you can address the highlights of the card, as well as the benefits it provides for your customers. You may already have a custom training program exclusively for the credit card, but in the "Sales Culture" program, reference the card, and emphasize its key features and benefits.

Any special customer promotions such as coupons, BOGO's (Buy One Get One offers), and rewards programs should be incorporated in the sales culture program as well. For service businesses, any VIP programs, loyalty or discount programs you offer to customers, as well as their key benefits, need to be included. In essence, anything that has to do with the selling side of your business, along with your company's selling philosophy, will play a part in this module.

Sales Techniques: Another program that is often mistaken as being part of customer service is "Sales Techniques." This program teaches the trainee the differences between proper and improper selling techniques, as well as how to qualify a customer. When qualifying a customer, the trainee will learn what types of open-ended questions to ask, and be given examples of commonly asked questions the customer may pose in return.

If you are truly committed to providing an excellent customer experience, then all sales obtained are deemed to be sales made by a "satisfied" customer. This means employees should not sell the customer needless merchandise or services, or mislead the customer in order to make a sale. An example of this futile selling technique would be a sales representative pressuring a customer into a sale, by saying, "you have to buy now, because the price is going up," when in reality the price is staying the same. When this occurs, customers realize they were deceived and become discontented. I have observed these practices among inexperienced or inadequately trained employees who feel they have to do whatever it takes to close the sale. To avoid lost sales, associates need to be shown appropriate sales methods.

Cumulatively, your customer service, sales culture, and sales techniques programs will provide your trainees with an ample understanding of how to successfully represent your business to your customers. All three programs should incorporate role-playing, so employees will have an opportunity to apply the skills they have acquired. When properly created and employed, these three programs are the foundation for a successful business and will help achieve The *Ultimate* Customer Experience.

Operations: It is highly unlikely you will cover all the information relevant to the topic of Operations within 30 minutes; therefore, you will need to break this down into several training modules. These training modules require a significant amount of hands-on training, and could include areas such as Point of Sale, Systems Training, and RF guns that utilize barcode training. People learn best by doing, so avoid using a manager or another employee to walk trainees through the process; instead, allow trainees to complete the practices themselves, which will be more valuable.

There are many training methods available today through the use of technology. These methods provide an opportunity for trainees to complete self-guided "hands-on" training, typically by setting the system to training mode. The use of "hands-on" training will allow employees to retain the information quickly and easily. A manager or another employee should be available to follow up with the trainee, to ensure he or she is properly operating the system. Trainees should learn as much as possible on their own, but ensure a manager is available if a problem arises.

Product Knowledge: Product knowledge is directly linked to sales; therefore, it is of equal importance to your customer service selling programs. The key goal of any product knowledge program is to supply employees with ample information about the product or service in order to intelligently discuss features and benefits. Employees should have sufficient knowledge of the products they are expected to sell in order to provide demonstrations when necessary, and make appropriate recommendations based on the customer's needs.

If you sell products or consumer services, allow your employees to engage in using them hands-on. The more familiar employees are with company products and services, the more capable they will be to sell with conviction. Make sure all product knowledge modules include sales techniques, as well as the key initiatives of your customer service program. Once your employees have mastered these training techniques, you will be pleasantly surprised with the increase in sales your company will obtain.

Merchandising: This program only relates to businesses that utilize goods displayed. A retail store, for example, must train employees on how to properly arrange merchandise on shelves or in window displays. Merchandise also needs to attract customers so they will be enticed to make a purchase. Employees need to also learn how to correctly tag or sticker items, price them, and arrange promotional signage. A restaurant uses signage throughout the year for new promotions, seasonal food menus, and specials for specific time periods. Even though merchandising is primarily task-driven, remember to explain to your employees why you are setting up displays or signage in a particular fashion, and what the value is to the customer, as well as to your business.

Safety: The goal of this program is to educate employees about your company's safety procedures. These procedures are essential when maintaining a safe environment for both the employee and the customer. Topics that should be included in this module will vary, depending on the type of business you operate. Some topics relevant to safety may include: protective clothing and footwear, appropriate use and storage of chemicals, how to carefully clean up spills and leaks, general lifting techniques, as well as proper evacuation and lock-down procedures. In addition, your business may have legal requirements that need to be met. If this is the case, make sure you understand your obligations and that you are in full compliance.

Management Skill Development: This training topic will encompass more than one module, covering subjects such as leadership, coaching, communication, organization, scheduling, payroll and more. Be clear with expectations for your managers, and create modules that include all materials necessary to perform their jobs effectively.

Make sure that all managers take your company's front-line employee training, so they will be competent in their management skills. Additionally, be certain that each management training module includes key fundamentals of your company's philosophy and your customer service objectives; include all applicable dynamics that set your business apart from the competition.

HR Issues/Associate Relations: When developing this training you may need to consult with an HR Specialist to determine the specific mandates for the state(s) you operate in. Some HR issues may include: recruiting employees, resolving conflicts, establishing and/or distributing benefits, and maintaining diversity. If you currently have insufficient training regarding your HR policies, determine what changes are necessary to fulfill the mandates. If necessary, consult an attorney to protect your business from any legal action that could be taken in the future.

If you truly want to achieve The *Ultimate* Customer Experience, the customer must be the focus of every training module, regardless of the topic, unless the customer is not physically present, which is hardly ever the case with front-line employees. Remember, as you develop your training modules, avoid the mistake made by many businesses: they do not include any information regarding the importance of the customer in training modules other than customer service.

An example of a topic where customer service may not be included in modules is POS training. POS stands for Point of Sale; it refers to the system that retailers and restaurants use for processing customer payments. Disappointingly, I have reviewed numerous new-hire training programs for POS terminals that do not include anything applicable to the customer or customer service.

There are many retail stores and fast-food restaurants where the only time the customer interacts with the employee is at the POS register. So, does it not make sense to include customer service topics within POS training? Of course it does, especially simple elements, such as greeting customers and thanking them for their purchase. However, when I have asked the question as to why these topics are not included, I am told, "We cover that in our customer service module." If you do not include customer significance in all of the training you provide, you will not be successful in creating a "customer first" environment.

In closing, training begins with creating an unmatched customer culture.

Providing excellent customer service is a priority for all businesses, and should not be viewed by an employer or an employee as a task or duty.

Chapter Eight

Training . . . What's Your Approach?

70% of buying experiences are based on how the customer feels they are being treated.—McKinsey

Companies rely on various resources to implement training. Some businesses invest in developing in-house training departments, while others choose to outsource their training. Additionally, there are companies that utilize a combination of both sources; for example, businesses may outsource special projects that cannot be handled internally. We will evaluate the advantages and disadvantages of each approach.

First, let's look at in-house training and its benefits. The advantages are usually obvious, such as the company maintaining control over its training, the ability to set deadlines, and deciding on methodologies. Another benefit to producing training internally, is the ability to make updates quickly and easily.

Now let's take a look at the disadvantages of in-house training. Internal trainers may not have the expertise to deliver high-quality training materials. If skill limitations are the issue, internal trainers will often create training methods they are most comfortable with. This is not always in the company's best interest. Some trainers are often unable to create valuable training, as they may lack the knowledge of what each company position entails, including manpower and time constraints.

Another downside to employing an internal training department is that some trainers hold full-time positions within the company, and they are required to create new training modules regularly; therefore, too many programs may be produced. This is often where "over-training" comes into play, as discussed in Chapter Six. Some trainers believe their sole position is to produce training programs. In addition, these trainers feel they should not be not held accountable when employees do not fully utilize the training provided. This type of mentality does not promote teamwork.

When our company performs an assessment for a business, one of the initiatives is to review their current training programs. We often find dull, lengthy training manuals; some employees may not have the time or aptitude to fully study them. We have also found low-quality videos and tedious on-line modules filled with heavy reading and/or PowerPoint slides, which do not capture the attention of the trainee. In general, we discovered a lot of in-house training lacks one key element: creativity. Remember, training should be fun, effective and engaging.

Bear in mind, I am not saying that every company who has an in-house training department is dealing with these types of issues; there are a number of companies out there who are providing substantial internal training. However, in my thirty years of experience working with all types and sizes of businesses, I have seen these issues take place with internal training more often than not.

Conversely, what happens if you outsource your training? Outsourcing can be very cost effective and allows companies to pick and choose vendors that will comply with their budget. Additionally, outside companies tend to be more knowledgeable concerning modern technology and strategic solutions. The use of cutting-edge technology also enhances tracking options for measuring training results.

Disadvantages such as inconsistency will occur when a company hires several different vendors to create training modules, each with a dissimilar look and feel. When inconsistency arises, it travels through the entire organization, and prevents trainees from grasping the information they need. All training modules must be relevant to one another; when multiple companies are producing the training, this will not occur.

The solution: employ a small, internal training department that identifies with the company's training needs. Hire an outside company that will partner with your internal staff, and utilize contemporary resources to produce successful training modules. This combination will allow you to better control your budget and scheduling needs.

In the last chapter, we discussed the ten most important training topics that front-line employees should be taught. Your next step is to break down company training goals and review the budget. In many businesses, often the larger portion of training dollars is spent on leadership and coaching for high level executives. As a result, fewer dollars will be available for front-line training. Trainers will be challenged as they allocate the remaining budget; they will need to determine from the list of training topics, which modules can be produced and delivered to front-line personnel.

Often training directors attempt to resolve budget-related issues by relying on their staff to utilize "buddy training" and "shadowing" methods. "Buddy training" involves a seasoned associate or manager working alongside a new hire, providing step-by-step instruction. "Shadowing" involves a new hire walking either alongside or behind an experienced employee throughout the workday. Both of these methods are not usually successful; let us look at why.

The first problem with both training methods is that individuals have their own style of explaining procedures and demonstrating task completion. Therefore the new hire is taught based on personal approach, as opposed to company standard. Factor in time constraints, personality issues, language barriers, along with high employee turnover, and you have a recipe for failure.

Keep in mind utilizing managers to train employees can be far more costly than delivering well-crafted training modules. Additionally, many businesses assume that managers can conduct training since they're already being paid, but in reality, the manager is taken away from attending to other important duties and tasks.

Years ago, my client, a housewares retail chain with 600 locations, was in need of several training modules. However, there was an urgency to create the product knowledge module for cookware first, due to a very disturbing incident that took place between a manager and a new hire. I was pleased to tell the client that all training programs would be in stores in just a few days. Again, the client mentioned product knowledge and proceeded to describe the situation that occurred, relating to the use of "buddy training."

The manager said,

"I know it's your first day and there's a lot you have to learn, but let me show you some of the cookware products we have." "Sure, okay," the new hire said, enthusiastically.

As the manager went through the various products and brands, he came to some products that apparently he did not appreciate, and said,

"We used to carry a really great brand but now we carry this *garbage* that I just don't like. The other brand was so much better."

The manager continued to show the rest of the products to the new hire, and continued to share his opinions. Can you imagine how the new hire must have felt on his first day in the store? What do you think happened to the new hire's enthusiasm for his job?

These types of situations occur when managers are forced to take the responsibility of training employees, and begrudgingly go through the motions.

Many managers prefer not to train new hires at all, although there may be some managers who truly enjoy it, and go about it with a positive attitude. By and large, asking managers to be your trainers will not provide the consistency needed in order to achieve The *Ultimate* Customer Experience.

Equally as ineffective as "buddy training" is "shadowing," which is commonly used in restaurants. We have all seen this when dining out, when two servers come to the table. One is usually observing, while the other greets the patron and takes the order. A drawback to "shadowing" is that the employee doing the training usually has a lower pay grade, less responsibility than a manager, and does not have a high level of commitment to the company. Therefore, the employee conducting the training does not possess the expertise, and worse yet, possibly the right attitude required to complete the training successfully. How can these employees ever deliver effective training when in so many cases they themselves did not receive proper training? This cycle continues to breed inconsistency company-wide.

I can recall two experiences while watching "shadowing" take place. Late one morning on the way to a meeting, I stopped in a local convenience store for a cup of coffee. I overheard a conversation between an employee who I knew had been working there for a while and one who was obviously a new hire. The conversation took place at the deli counter as the employee was showing the new hire how to make sandwiches.

This is what I heard:

"We're supposed to weigh the cold cuts before putting them on the sandwich to make sure they're the right weight, but I just put on three slices. It's usually about the same."

As a result, this employee has now taken the liberty to ignore corporate policy and just assume that three slices are enough. What stood out in my mind the most were the radio commercials advertising that this chain sets itself apart from competitors by giving more ounces of meat per sandwich. So does the new hire weigh the cold cuts before putting them on the sandwich or does the new hire follow the seasoned employee's instructions?

The second experience occurred when stopping in a restaurant for lunch one day while traveling between two meetings. The new hire, Amy, greeted me while the employee she was "shadowing," Brad, stood behind her. Amy warmly greeted me, and I immediately complimented her and congratulated her on her new job. Here's what surprised me: Brad at one time came over to my table alone to refill my glass. I asked him how the training was going; he told me he hated it and was looking forward to Friday because it was his last day. It was already Wednesday, and I couldn't believe that the restaurant manager chose an employee who was leaving and unhappy with his job, to train a new hire. Does that make sense?

When they both returned, I asked Amy if she was ready to take over for Brad, who was leaving. She looked concerned because she did not know who would continue to train her, and apparently Brad did a fine job of letting Amy know how much he hated the job - as well as what she is most likely going to have to deal with. Amy's words were most disappointing to me because she seemed to be eager to do well with her new job. She said,

"Well, based on what I've heard from Brad, I don't know how long I am going to survive here anyway. He told me they deduct our pay for every mistake."

Brad just smiled as if to say Amy should not have said that. Amy asked if I wanted anything else, and when I said "no," she proceeded to hand me my check. I wished her luck and they both walked away. I would have liked to return to that restaurant a week or so later to see how Amy was doing, but I was on a road trip and did not expect to be back there any time soon.

Nevertheless, the point here is to think twice before delegating the important responsibility of training employees to either managers or other employees. More often than not, companies will be spending more dollars on ineffective practices, and will need to spend even more in the future to undo the damage these methods can cause.

In addition, there are trainers who rely heavily on video. High-quality video production is labor intensive and costly, and often requires hiring an outside company to script, shoot, and edit. Companies may not always have the budget to support high-quality video production; therefore, they tend to create poor-quality in-house training videos. Consequently, trainees become frustrated and find it impossible to learn, as these videos often contain outdated and irrelevant material that does not accurately represent their job description.

Another method of delivery businesses utilize is e-learning, also known as online training. This is typically more cost-effective to produce and maintain. In-house training departments produce these modules themselves, but frequently lack creativity. Heavily text-driven PowerPoint slides, along with the use of poor quality audio, hinder retention.

So before you invest in training, assess your goals, review your budget and determine which delivery methods are best for your company. If this is your first venture in providing employee training, there are various approaches to consider.

Let's recap the different options available:

Written Materials:

If your budget and staff are limited, written training materials are an affordable option. Yet, if this is the only means you have to provide training, be certain that what is written clearly defines the message you're attempting to convey. Managers who utilize written training materials must remember to avoid thick manuals filled with "Do's" and "Do Not's." Do not expect employees to memorize lengthy text, instead use straighforward concepts to explain the information. Make it easy for employees to comprehend "What" they need to learn, by explaining "Why" they need to understand it. This will allow employees to embrace your vision and bring it to fruition.

When using written materials, managers should create opportunities for employees to participate in group discussions, whereby they can offer input. You may find that some of the best ideas come from employees, so be open-minded to their suggestions.

Generic Programs:

Generic training materials may not be the best choice to represent your business. Customizing training materials are very important, so think twice about purchasing "off-the-shelf" training. Nevertheless, if you must purchase a generic training program, look for something that is close to what you wish employees to learn. It's also important that you "screen" these outside materials before passing them on to your employees. In addition, consider enhancing the program by including a customized piece, such as a pamphlet.

For example, suppose you purchased a generic video that discusses customer service. The video uses standard greetings such as "good morning," or, "good afternoon"; however your company has a specific greeting for your employees to use when welcoming customers or answering the phone. Supplement the video with a short one or two page pamphlet that addresses the generic video's key points, and insert any specifics relevant to your own customer service program. Your pamphlet should explain WHY customers must be addressed with your custom greeting line, and WHY you believe it will help provide quality customer service.

Videos:

As mentioned earlier, producing quality video requires competence and a sizeable budget. If limited funds are preventing you from hiring an outside company to professionally produce your training videos, think twice before you take it upon yourself to create in-house versions. Delivering low-quality videos sends the wrong message to your employees. Videos should reflect your business culture, which is something you want your employees to embrace.

Nevertheless, if using in-house video is essential, retain a freelance videographer and editor who share your objectives. To keep costs down, make the video brief; a well-produced short video will suffice.

PowerPoint:

PowerPoint is a slide-based program used to create dynamic presentations for an audience. Presentation slides support a live presentation in which each slide is interpreted through the use of text, graphics, music, narrative and animation. This program is traditionally used for business presentations, however when utilizing it as a training tool, different formats apply.

PowerPoint slides used within a training module should use text sparingly and allow images to tell the story. Avoid long boring presentations with countless slides, and use sub-topics to further break down topics when necessary. When utilizing text, keep it straightforward and easy to read. Graphics can further illustrate your presentations, and animation can be used for emphasis. If you choose to record a narrative, select a narrator who has a pleasant vocal tone, can read well, and use proper inflection and intonation. Moreover, if you are compelled to use background music, select music that is upbeat and will hold your employees' interest.

Classroom:

Should you decide that classroom-style training is your best option, be selective when choosing an instructor. The classroom instructor can position your training to either succeed or fail. Select an instructor who is a skilled motivator with excellent teaching abilities, and has a pleasant personality. Remember, your primary goal is to provide trainees with the information they need to successfully perform their job responsibilities. When teaching, instuctors need to provide clear explanations of all procedures and why they need to be performed.

Maintain brief classroom sessions and avoid veering off curriculum topics. Classroom training needs to be interactive; instructors should get input and feedback from traineees, same as they do when written training materials are used. To support trainees further, instructors should develop follow-up sessions to reinforce the skills learned, whereby trainees can apply what they've learned in their work environment.

Now that you have explored the various training options available, let's discuss the role a Director or Manager of Training may have in delivering training. Trainers tend to use training methods that allow them to maintain their comfort level, and also fit within their budget constraints. To obtain maximum results, regardless of what training method you choose, each training module should present opportunities for trainees to actively participate. For example, if you are using video training, be certain to include activities, exercises, and role-plays to supplement the video. Although various topics may require different training methods, all programs must relate to one another and require trainee participation.

To conclude this chapter, we will summarize what was previously discussed regarding training.

Whomever you select to create training for your business, he or she must remember to keep training materials short, engaging and fun. Every training program produced, regardless of methodology, must be relevant to one another and include elements of your business culture. Trainees will eagerly embrace training if it is beneficial to them, as well as enjoyable.

Once training has been implemented, follow-up with employees to determine if they found it helpful and what they learned from it. Get their feedback on what could be done to improve the training going forward. View any negative feedback as a valuable tool that will allow you to make changes for the better in upcoming programs. Test employees after training has been taken to get a general idea of the effectiveness of your training; if you have a high percentage of employees who did not score well, use this opportunity to consider revising the training and what you are trying to accomplish.

Training needs to be updated on an continual basis. Businesses make changes frequently, and training needs to reflect those adjustments. If you are using outdated training, you will not obtain the results you are striving for. Keep training up-to-date, in accordance with the changes your business has gone through.

If you find that your first attempt at producing training has not yielded the desired results, you can improve it easily. Continually listen to what your employees are telling you, and take their needs to heart. Once you master the techniques that work best for your business, you will have the means to deliver productive training and meet your company's goals.

Remember, training is a partnership between employer and employee, with both sides working together. Place equal value on your employees' input; you WILL achieve outstanding results.

Make all of your training the best it can be. And, most importantly, be sure to incorporate the customer experience in every program, by including this vital message: "There is no one, or nothing, more important than the customer."

Chapter Nine

Training:
Cost * Evaluation * ROI

68% of customer defection takes place because customers feel poorly treated.
Source: TARP

Companies that invest in training do so with the hope of solving problems and becoming more productive. One would think that investing in training would lead a company to great success. Unfortunately, when looking at all that is involved with training, more often than not, this isn't the case. Training has become a multi-billion dollar industry consisting of various types of programs and technology.

So the next question to ask yourself is, "What will effective training cost my company?" Training is not easily measured. There is often a misconception of the dollar investment on paper and what training is actually costing a company after it has been implemented. Training is not measured in the same way other costs are determined, such as advertising.

According to Chron Small Business, many companies find it easier to take a set portion of their sales revenue, typically between two and five percent, and invest it in advertising. This is a tangible number that can be measured against a return-on-investment (ROI), depending on the advertising results. ROI can be easily calculated when all cost factors are evident, and a specific tracking system is in place. For example, a single operation spent $15,000 on a three-day promotional ad, which utilized a coupon to track the promotion's success. The ad attracted 200 additional customers with an average sale of $100 per customer. Based on these figures the company generated a total of $20,000 in sales from the ad. Subtracting the cost of the ad, the company earned an additional $5000 in sales, which gave them approximately a 33% ROI. Obviously, the ROI will be somewhat lower when the cost of the overhead is factored in.

When it comes to training, companies allocate a significantly lower percentage, which is typically one percent or less of total sales. Let's take a look at an example of budget allocation for a $500 million retail chain that has an in-house training department, but also utilizes "buddy training." We discussed the issues with "buddy training" in Chapter Eight. This retail chain's in-house training department consists of three people: a training director, manager and an assistant. The salaries and benefits of these three employees could cost $300,000 or more. The company also allocates a $300,000 training budget, divided between store personnel and executive training. Executive training typically takes the lion's share, so perhaps out of the $300,000 there is only $100,000 left for store level training.

With such a small budget, the in-house training department relies heavily on manual training, conducted by in-store managers who also employ "buddy training." The in-house department most likely will write the training manuals and outsource the printing, which is another cost to factor in. In addition to the manuals, the in-house training department might attempt to produce one or two inexpensive, low-quality videos totaling $20,000 or $30,000. Additionally, the video duplication for 500 stores could cost another $1500-$2000.

The Chief Financial Officer looks at the budget and only sees the $300,000 training cost, which is *less than one percent* of the retail chain's sales. Conversely, the number that is greatly overlooked, because it is not a line item, is the payroll spent on managers conducting the training, because it is simply part of the overhead.

If the manager earns $15.00 per hour and the store level associate earns $7.50 per hour, the business spends $22.50 per hour for training. The argument often made is that managers are being paid anyway so it's no problem for them to do the training. In reality, when relying heavily on "buddy training," the managers are pulled away from doing more productive tasks for the business, and that is costing dollars, and in many cases, sales. Consider this: If a manager spends three hours training an employee, that is costing the business $45.00 in payroll and the time could have been spent on the manager's daily responsibilities. When you multiply that number times the number of employees, the aggregate number of hours, and the total number of stores, that number will soon be in the hundreds of thousands.

This is also causing major disconnect within the business, which ultimately costs the company additional dollars. As we discussed in Chapter Eight, when relying on managers to conduct training, they tend to incorporate their own personal experiences and training methods. I am not saying that managers do not have a role with new or existing employees, however their time should be balanced accordingly. Managers play a supporting role with all employees; they should assist employees when necessary, answer questions and take part in role-playing exercises. When managers are able to complete their daily tasks, payroll dollars will be more productive and training will be consistent and effective.

So how do you measure training and more importantly, how can you conclude if your investment is giving you an effective ROI? Typically trainers will use test scores to measure the success of their training programs. Alas, test scores *will not* provide an ROI.

Although testing can be useful, keep in mind that trainees can achieve high-test scores and still not apply what they have learned to their job. Why? Trainers use high test scores to exemplify successful training. Unfortunately, high-test scores do not always translate into competent skill application. At times training questions are too easy, or employees ask other co-workers for the answer. In some cases, the manager actually gives the answers to the trainee so that the manager appears to be qualified in hiring talented people. If this is the case, obviously the training is not successful for the company.

The following is an example of a company that was experiencing serious performance issues while using test scores to measure training. I entered into contract with them and performed an assessment to locate disconnect. In the meeting there were several executives from operations, finance, and training. The operations executives had to deal with customer complaints, performance issues, and lackluster sales. However, when we began to discuss their training, the Vice President of Training was thrilled to share his test scores, which was all he had.

When I asked him questions about how their training measured up to actual performance and sales results, he said it was not necessary to discuss because training was not the problem. When I asked him why he felt that way, he answered, "Because we get high test scores."

Following the completion of our assessment, we looked further into the matter and found that the training this company provided allowed for their employees to share answers; in many cases, the trainees only took the tests and did not take the actual training. Naturally, this was an easy problem for us to fix. We completely revamped their training using our patented methodology; we developed testing that employees could only answer correctly if they took the training, and we carefully monitored and measured results. Within six months, their customer complaints dropped by 80% and sales were up 12.5%. Much to my surprise, the Vice President of Training became our best friend when he saw what we were accomplishing. Unfortunately, years later the company was bought by a private investment firm, management was changed, and within two years the company went out of business. However, during the five years we worked with them, the company quickly became more productive and sales dramatically increased.

Every type of training program or module is measurable, and is vital for the success of any business. Set goals and use formulas that will accurately measure how well the training is being applied to the job it was designed for.

Training results may vary, but as a general guideline you should see positive results within the following timeframes:

Product training is fairly easy to measure. If successful, the business should see an increase in sales on the product(s) within 30-60 days after the training rollout. Successful training for selling techniques will show an increase in conversion rates also within 30-60 days after roll out.

Point of Sale (POS) training for cashiers operating a register would prove successful based on accurate register balance, as well as a reduction in the total number of times the manager is contacted to perform system overrides. Improvements should be seen immediately after training is completed. After 15-30 days, a new hire should be successful at operating the register system.

Safety training on the other hand, may be somewhat challenging to measure. For example, a company with a high number of accidents who recently implemented safety training, or revised its current program, may or may not witness an immediate change. However over a short period of time, as the trainees have adapted to the new safety procedures, the company should see a measureable decrease in the number of incidents.

After training is completed for all or any of these topics and there is little or no improvement, your training proved ineffective and you should consider revising your training techniques.

Now let us take a look at how investing in various training investments (not training scores) can produce a disappointing ROI:

Heavily investing in technology is a good example. When used properly, technology is an excellent tool. However, many times after it is purchased, the technology sits idle without being utilized to its full potential. For example, if a company invests in a Learning Management System (LMS) that costs $250,000 or more, dollars will be wasted if the system is used incorrectly, or not used at all. One way to avoid this problem is to be sure a company purchases the correct LMS for their business, one with a user-friendly system.

In addition to overspending on Learning Management Systems, companies invest heavily in PC training terminals, as well as tablets and mobile applications. These tools can be very successful for training purposes, but only if they are accompanied by effective training modules.

Another expense occurs when companies contract with e-learning platform companies. These companies allow in-house trainers to utilize the e-learning company's tools such as their LMS, generic modules and sometimes, custom modules. These modules are often created by the trainers or through very limited options offered by the e-learning company. This type of program becomes very costly because businesses are paying a licensing fee for every trainee and every module they use. Unfortunately, this type of program yields very limited success.

An additional waste of time and money can occur when a business invests in its own video production studio. This is rare, but businesses that have the financial ability to make this type of investment utilize in-house videos as a main source of training. Some of these businesses have gone so far as to have their own in-house TV network with monitors at their locations, allowing employees to watch videos before or after business hours. During off-hours it may be challenging for employees to focus on training and absorb the material covered in the videos. Also these videos can be extremely brief, change topics frequently and often do not tie into key initiatives.

The last training investment mistake that we will discuss involves a training method that combines classroom-style training conducted by field trainers. Assembling all participants into one setting sounds ideal and a modified version may work in some situations. However, in most cases the issues we discussed regarding classroom training, combined with travel expenses, often do not justify the cost. So before investing in this method and implementing it throughout your entire organization, test it beforehand, to prove its effectiveness.

Simply said, you *can* measure training results—it is no different than any other part of your business. First, look at what your training department is providing your employees. Find out if the training delivered is meeting your goals and expectations. Evaluate your sales and training reports to determine if there is a direct correlation between those numbers and your revenue and conversion increases. Focus specifically on your product training, along with customer service and sales training. Lastly, remember when calculating ROI, you must factor in revenue, the cost of training module(s), methods of facilitation, along with training payroll expenses.

Do not be afraid to hold your trainers accountable. Granted, if training rolls out and there is no support from managers or other departments such as operations, then the trainers should not be held accountable. However, if corporate policy mandates that employees are to use the programs in-house trainers have created, those trainers are 100% responsible for delivering effective, on-time modules. Bottom line: unless you receive positive results, training has failed and changes must be made.

Chapter Ten

It's ALL Up To You

Customer loyalty can be worth up to 10 times as much as a single purchase.
Source: the White House Office of Consumer Affairs, Washington, DC.

As the owner or manager of your business, you have the opportunity to create a successful environment. This book has provided you with necessary steps to help your business flourish and achieve the *Ultimate* Customer Experience . . . you CAN make it happen.

Let's recap and make sure you didn't miss anything. Did you perform the assessment for your company? What did your findings reveal about your business? Remember to re-do the assessment at least every three years to ensure your company stays focused and aligned with your vision and goals.

Consistency is vital. Maintain consistency within corporate and field communication, training methods, policies, procedures and all other areas of your company. This is key in building a successful business. Lack of consistency is the number one cause of disconnect, and as we have discussed, disconnect destroys businesses and hinders them from reaching their full potential. Did you follow the steps for eliminating disconnect, and have you implemented them into your business?

Establishing and maintaining the right culture for your business also plays a large role in eliminating disconnect. As you daily manage your business, culture consistency is something that you must always focus on. Have you evaluated the culture of your business? Is it the type of culture you are proud of? Are you treating your employees fairly, giving constructive criticism when necessary and providing them opportunities to grow within your company? If not, are you taking the proper steps to improve it? Keep your eye on your culture and look for any signs that may tell you it is changing negatively. If it is, repair it immediately to avoid a downward spiral.

As discussed in Chapter Three, it is imperative your business provides one consistent message, both externally and internally, so customers and employees are not confused. Make sure you stay connected with your advertising campaigns, and ensure your customers can easily receive offer(s) as they interact with front-line employees. To evaluate your customer service program, "Mystery Shop" your business periodically. The larger your company, the more frequently you should conduct mystery shops. As a customer of your own business, you will be able to judge how well your employees are providing customer service and what improvements you may need to make.

As we discussed in Chapter Four, do not fall into the trap of believing that customers do their own research and therefore do not need professional assistance when choosing a product or service. Make sure your employees are courteous, and provide accurate information regarding the merchandise and services you provide. This will help increase sales and prompt satisfied customers to tell everyone they know about your business. This free advertising will bring in even more customers.

Lastly, when training employees, find the right balance between providing education and information, but do not over-train. Make sure you provide fun and engaging training that employees can easily learn from, and retain what they learn when applying those skills to their jobs. Support training initiatives, as well as all of your managers and senior staff. It will become part of your culture and when you implement training properly, your employees will utilize it and productivity will increase.

Achieving outstanding customer service is possible, but no one said it would be easy. It does take great effort at first, but eventually with the right steps, superb customer service will happen naturally and your customers will respond favorably.

To sum it up simply: maintain a positive culture, run your business with consistency, take care of your employees, and use your own passion every day as the driving force for your success. You will have the winning formula to eliminate disconnect and take your business to the next level.

Remember, it all starts with the most important, yet simple rule: "there is no one, or nothing, more important than the customer." If you remember and agree with this statement, and follow what we have discussed throughout this book, your business will begin the most exciting journey—one filled with growth, profit and vast success!

In closing, do you remember John, the consumer in the Introduction, and the result of his shopping experience? He needed to purchase a specific item, which was only available at that store. Unfortunately, John has no choice but to once again return to the store he vowed never to go back to. Let's find out what happened when John reluctantly returned to that same store for another purchase:

It is Saturday morning. John has been thinking about this item all week and is looking forward to finally purchasing it, but he is dreading going back to that store again. He gets up, showers, gets dressed, has a light breakfast and heads to the mall. He is thrilled to find a place to park and it's still early, so the mall is not yet crowded. John heads into the store hoping he can find the item himself, and is completely caught off guard when a friendly store associate greets him immediately. Shocked but pleased, John smiles at the associate and says, "hello" back to the person. They begin talking and the store associate tells John where to find the item, but just like the last time, John cannot find it.

Hmm . . . looking around for help, he sees that dreaded door that reads "Employees Only," but this time an associate coming out of that door, and walks over to assist him,

"Hi, can I help you find something?"

John is speechless! He tells the associate what he is looking for, but that he cannot find it. The associate smiles at John and escorts him to the proper area where the merchandise is located. Then the store associate explains that their store did carry a few models of that particular brand, but some customers returned them because they were dissatisfied with the item. Much to John's delight, the store associate suggests a different brand and explains why this item is superior.

John pauses for a moment, listens to the associate, and decides it makes sense to purchase the item. Before walking to the register, the associate also suggests to John two additional items that will complement his purchase, and provide additional benefits. John's last visit was quite a while ago, and he is in shock with the many improvements that have been implemented. In fact, John is so pleased with what he has witnessed that he agrees to make additional purchases. Still in a state of disbelief, John continues to glance at the door marked, "Employees Only." He can't believe associates are no longer running for cover, to avoid making contact with the enemy (*the customer*).

Finally, the associate escorts John to the register. Once there, another friendly associate suggests to John that he should sign up for the Store's "Customer Rewards Program" and explains the benefits he will receive. John is thrilled with the store, the purchases he made, and the service he received. He wonders if there are hidden cameras somewhere and he is appearing on a show like "Undercover Boss." John is beginning to realize that this store has corrected its customer service issues . . . but he doesn't know that these improvements have resulted from applying the principles in this book. Now, John eagerly signs up for the Customer Rewards Program and he will become an extremely loyal customer.

And there you have it . . . this store has achieved . . . The *Ultimate* Customer Experience.

Congratulations . . . you are now on your way to achieving The *Ultimate* Customer Experience and accomplishing all of your goals. Good luck!

About the Author

Art Suriano, CEO of The TSi Company, has nearly thirty-five years of experience in business, beginning his career in musical composition. At the age of 19, Suriano was composing music for NBC Daytime Soap Operas: "Another World," "The Guiding Light," and "As The World Turns." He has composed music scores and commercials for brands such as Ford, Subaru, AT&T, Ricoh, and Prudential. In 1985, Suriano started his first business by writing jingles and buying radio time for his retail clients. Within two years, the company grew into a full-service advertising agency with annual revenue reaching over 2 million dollars; and at the five-year mark, the agency was bringing in over 5 million annually.

During the 1990's, most of Suriano's Ad Agency clients were retailers who were hit hard by the recession. These clients were looking for a new avenue of survival, so Suriano began to focus more heavily on "radio marketing." He began consulting for WABC-AM in New York, and KISS 108 in Boston. Learning more about radio from the inside, Suriano began to develop ideas of how to bring the success of radio into other areas of business.

After years of writing music, scripts, commercials and creating promotions, Suriano came up with the idea of utilizing radio for retailers and created a custom radio format called RadioPlus™. The concept was used as an in-store marketing program, which also sparked the birth of The TSi Company. RadioPlus™ was very successful. However, he soon saw a greater need among retailers and began providing highly effective training solutions for store level associates. Within a few years, Suriano's new training concept became a patented methodology known as LTraining®, serving over 3 million users to date and scoring over 90% retention after a single session. LTraining® became so successful that Suriano expanded TSi into a full-service solution provider.

Today, The TSi Company works with companies large and small, which represent various industries such as retail, service, hospitality and more. TSi clients have experienced improvement in sales, marketing, communication, technology, company culture and training. Some of these clients have also been featured in the Top 100 Industry Leaders List.

Suriano has been happily married for over 32 years and has two wonderful children.